The Brutalist

A black and white montage of architectural elements; a flurry of shapes, curves, angles, and shadows.

INSERT TITLE:

OVERTURE

CUE: The sonic boom of a ship's hull impacting against the waves; each redundant crash gives way to a romantic orchestral swell...

1   **INT. INTERVIEW ROOM IN VAS COUNTY - MORNING LIGHT**   1

NOTE: Ocean waves fight the diegetic audio for duration of scene.

CLOSE ON -

A haunted and brutalized young woman, **ZSÓFIA**, is isolated in the frame. A vast European landscape can be viewed through the casement windows behind her.

>   BORDER OFFICER (O.S.)
>   (Hungarian)
>   *Your escort is right outside. She tells us that you are her niece. Are you her niece? Is she your aunt? Where is your mother? Is she alive? Do you know? Do you understand me when I speak? Do you prefer English or Czech?*

No response.

>   BORDER OFFICER (CONT'D)
>   *If you are from Budapest as the lady says, may you please state the name and street number of your former place of residence for the record? There's a pen and piece of paper in front of you... If you prefer not to speak to us, we suggest you write it down along with your family name, and we will take it upon ourselves to try and confirm this. Do you remember that address?*

No response.

>   BORDER OFFICER (CONT'D)
>   *Is it possible the woman outside is not related to you at all, but simply an ally you made along the way who is trying to help you? You bear little resemblance to one another. We will not punish her for trying to help an innocent young woman. We want to help you get home. Your true home. What is your true home? Help us to help you get home.*

CUE: DIEGETIC AUDIO FADES OUT...

> ERZSÉBET (V.O.)
> (Hungarian)
> *László, I am alive. Attila tells me that you, **too**, are alive and en route to him from Bremerhaven. Rejoice!*

CUE: Violins shriek.

CROSS DISSOLVE:

2 **INT. SHIP - LOWER DECK - DUSK** 2

It's dark but slowly our eyes adjust like a developing photograph hung to dry from a chemical bath.

A SERIES OF ANGLES -

Guided by the ocean's current beneath them; slumbering men, women, and children rock back and forth in their bunk beds.

> ERZSÉBET (V.O.)
> (Hungarian)
> *I cried out in ecstasy to have news of you. Zsófia is with me though she is frail, strange and quite ill. We anxiously await our being repatriated, but recently she has not been herself which has, in turn, roused unnecessary suspicions with local officials.*

CLOSE, ULTRA-BOWED LENS ON -

LÁSZLÓ TOTH, malnourished with a badly broken nose. He has the face of an emigrant.

A door opens off-screen and light pours in. Several bodies wipe the frame. A fellow **HUNGARIAN REFUGEE** shakes LÁSZLÓ by his shoulder. **LÁSZLÓ slaps his hand in response, shooting upwards violently.**

> HUNGARIAN REFUGEE
> (*Hungarian*)
> *Documents...*

LÁSZLÓ regains composure, wipes sleep from his eye. The light blooming from off-screen is transcendent.

> ERZSÉBET (V.O.)
> (Hungarian)
> *Fortunately, a few Soviet boys have taken a liking to us. They pity your poor niece especially who has grown fuller, even lovelier, since you last set eyes on her. These lonesome young servicemen are ostensibly entranced by such a radiant creature's commitment to absolute silence.*

LÁSZLÓ searches for his things in a panic. He looks to the
man off-screen.

>   LÁSZLÓ
>   (Hungarian)
>   *WHERE ARE MY THINGS?*
>
>   HUNGARIAN REFUGEE (O.S.)
>   (Hungarian)
>   *WHAT?*
>
>   LÁSZLÓ
>   (Hungarian)
>   *IT IS NOT AMUSING TO ME! WHERE IS
>   MY LUGGAGE?!*

LÁSZLÓ pushes the man off-screen who breaks into a fit of
laughter.

>   HUNGARIAN REFUGEE
>   (Hungarian)
>   Oh, stop it! Don't look at me that
>   way, old man! It's tucked there
>   under the mattress!

LÁSZLÓ ducks down to find a large canvas bag and pulls it
out.

>   ERZSÉBET (V.O.)
>   (Hungarian)
>   *The Soviets have helped us relocate
>   to a nearby shelter for displaced
>   persons near Vas. They encourage us
>   to "enjoy our freedoms," but I am
>   reminded of Goethe; "None are more
>   hopelessly enslaved than those who
>   falsely believe themselves free!" I
>   make no mistake, we are not yet
>   free.*
>
>   HUNGARIAN REFUGEE
>   (Hungarian)
>   Hurry László, or we'll be last in
>   the queue.

LÁSZLÓ and the refugee fight their way through the crowded
space towards the increasingly overwhelming sunlight,
throwing off our camera's white balance.

>   ERZSÉBET (V.O.)
>   (Hungarian)
>   *You, like myself, must be
>   envisioning so many terribly awful,
>   <u>awful</u> things but it is better that
>   your thoughts not get the best of
>   you.*

3   **INT. SHIP - STAIRWELL - CONTINUOUS**   3

They squeeze through a narrow doorway and up three flights of
stairs.

> ERZSÉBET (V.O.)
> *It is neither better, nor worse than you might imagine. I have kept myself _mostly_ to myself. More importantly, I have defended Zsófia from unwanted advances.*

The ferocious energy builds to a crescendo.

4   **EXT. SHIP DECK - CONTINUOUS**   4

The two men reach the top of the stairwell to the upper deck where dozens of immigrants take their place.

> ERZSÉBET (V.O.)
> *Below is the address I am told for mail in Vas. Please write to me at once when you have received this.*

The camera whip-pans over and up to the Statue of Liberty at a peculiar LOW-ANGLE.

> ERZSÉBET (V.O.)
> (Hungarian)
> *I am certain now that there is nothing left for us here. Go to America and I will follow you.*

LÁSZLÓ and the man beside him squeeze each other by the arm.

> ERZSÉBET (V.O.
> *Faithfully, Erzsébet.*

CUE: Strings and tympany reach a climax.

INSERT TITLE:

PART ONE
THE ENIGMA OF ARRIVAL
1947-1952

5   **INT. HIAS CENTER BASEMENT - NIGHT**   5

TWO HIAS REPRESENTATIVES (Hebrew Immigrant Aid Society) wearing unassuming dark coats and hats address a room crowded with Jewish émigré wearing numbered cards around their necks. One representative speaks in English, the other translates simultaneously over the speech in Yiddish.

HIAS REPRESENTATIVE (English) -for those of you who do not speak English, please engage myself or any of my colleagues located at the back so we may inform you about our orientation and language programs which are provided in this very room - 425 Lafayette - remember that address. Additionally, classes and daily meetings are held where many of you will be staying tonight over at the Hotel Marseilles located on 103rd and Broadway.	HIAS REPRESENTATIVE 2 (Yiddish) *-for those of you who do not speak English, please engage myself or any of my colleagues located at the back so we may inform you about our orientation and language programs which are provided in this room - 425 Lafayette - remember that address. Additionally, classes and daily meetings are held where many of you will be staying tonight over at the Hotel Marseilles located on 103rd and Broadway.*

It's difficult to discern LÁSZLÓ amongst the other faces in the crowd.

HIAS REPRESENTATIVE (CONT'D) (English) And for those of you of which none of the aforementioned details apply and who are immediately departing for other destinations in the morning, please see me about your $25 travel-aid.	HIAS REPRESENTATIVE 2 (CONT'D) (Yiddish) *And for those of you of which none of that applies and who are immediately departing for other destinations in the morning, please see us about a $25 travel-aid.*

One HIAS REPRESENTATIVE holds up and demonstrates a travel voucher.

                    HIAS REPRESENTATIVE (CONT'D)
These vouchers are redeemable for both trains and participating bus services.

CUE: Mournful solo piano plays over all of the following until otherwise noted.

EXT. NYC EAST RIVER DOCKS - NIGHT

LONG LENS ON -

A foghorn blows over a slow pan across a few girls talking amongst themselves while vying for some local business.

INT. BROTHEL - LATER

A woman performs intense oral sex on the HUNGARIAN REFUGEE who leans against an armoir in the background. In the foreground, a **PROSTITUTE** knelt on the floor tries to arouse LÁSZLÓ, though his penis remains flaccid in her grip.

                    PROSTITUTE
          Don't you think I'm beautiful?

LÁSZLÓ appears stoic, uncomfortable, or perhaps somewhat conflicted.

                    LÁSZLÓ
          I do-

                    PROSTITUTE
          Which parts of me do you find most
          beautiful? Is there a part of me
          you would especially like to touch
          or look at?

                    LÁSZLÓ
          -all parts.

                    PROSTITUTE
              (affects seduction)
          Stop it. I don't find all the parts
          of you beautiful. There are some
          parts of you which I like very
          much.

                    HUNGARIAN REFUGEE (O.S.)
          Fuck her!

LÁSZLÓ's girl is annoyed at his friend's outburst.

                    PROSTITUTE
          Can you tell your friend to be
          polite?

LÁSZLÓ shouts back in Hungarian.

                    LÁSZLÓ
              (Hungarian)
          Keep your mouth shut.

                    PROSTITUTE
          Which parts do you find ugly?

She's moved to LÁSZLÓ's neck to try kissing him romantically. Still, no response.

                    PROSTITUTE (CONT'D)
          My breasts?

                    LÁSZLÓ
          No, they are beautiful.

                    PROSTITUTE
          My legs? Are they too thin?

LÁSZLÓ struggles to find the correct adjective in English.

                    LÁSZLÓ
          You are- well-proportioned.

He squeezes her thighs below frame.

                    PROSTITUTE
          Well-proportioned? Well, I think
          that just made my day.

She presses harder now against him.

                    PROSTITUTE (CONT'D)
          My arse; is that what you like? You
          think it's beautiful?

                    LÁSZLÓ
          Very... It's the space above your
          brow for me which is the problem-

She stops, taken aback.

                    PROSTITUTE
          What?

                    LÁSZLÓ
          That's something I do not like.

                    PROSTITUTE
               (without affect)
          Your face is ugly.

                    LÁSZLÓ
               (despondent)
          I know it is.

8   **INT. BROTHEL HALLWAY - LATER**   8

The **MADAME** waits for LÁSZLÓ as he exits the room.

                    MADAME
          We have boys if you prefer.
          Brothers with dark skin but
          handsome. We can call for them.

                    LÁSZLÓ
          No, thank you.

                    MADAME
          Stay awhile. We have a movie on
          tonight.

                    LÁSZLÓ
          Excuse me?

                    MADAME
          We have a special movie on the
          projector downstairs. Comes free of
          charge with a glass of champagne.

9   **INT. BROTHEL BASEMENT - MOMENTS LATER**   9

A gramophone blasts classical music which fights the still
persistent non-diegetic solo piano.

LÁSZLÓ enters a makeshift home cinema holding a glass of
champagne where some silent pornography (circa 1930) is being
projected.

10   **EXT. CHINATOWN - DAWN**   10

LONG LENS ON -

LÁSZLÓ and the HUNGARIAN REFUGEE run for their lives to catch
a departing bus. The two drunks bang on its door and the bus
stops. They embrace each other like brothers and LÁSZLÓ steps
on-board leaving his friend behind him.

11   **EXT. BUS - DAY**   11

CUE: Stravinsky continues.

ULTRA-WIDE LOW ANGLE ON -

Asphalt rushes at us. The midday gloom hangs heavy.

A SERIES OF ANGLES ON -

- A sign reads, **"WELCOME TO PHILADELPHIA - Enjoy Our Past,
Experience Our Future!"**

- driving view of Philadelphia City Hall (constructed 1901)

- driving view of the Philadelphia Museum of Art (constructed
1928)

- driving view of the first International style skyscraper,
the Philadelphia Savings Fund Society building (constructed
1932)

- driving view of Pennsylvania Station, 30th Street
(constructed 1933)

12   **INT. BUS - LATER**   12

LÁSZLÓ rests his head against the frosted window.

LÁSZLÓ'S VIEW FROM BUS WINDOW -

A heavy snow comes down on LÁSZLÓ's cousin, **ATTILA**, who
stands amongst a group of on-lookers awaiting visitors
expectedly.

13   **EXT. BUS / DOWNTOWN PHILADELPHIA - MOMENTS LATER**   13

ATTILA holds his blood relative in an intense embrace.

                          ATTILA
                Cousin.

8.

                    LÁSZLÓ
          Cousin.

                    ATTILA
          Erzsébet is alive.

LÁSZLÓ's knees buckle, deeply moved.

                    LÁSZLÓ
          What did you say?

ATTILA switches to Hungarian.

                    ATTILA
               (Hungarian)
          *I have a letter from her - your
          Erzsébet is alive and she is with
          little Zsófia.*

LÁSZLÓ lets out a deep emotional wail and holds his blood relative tight in his arms.

14   **INT. FURNITURE SHOWROOM - LATER**   14

TRACK WITH -

ATTILA and his young American wife, **AUDREY**, show LÁSZLÓ around the shop. ATTILA rambles nervously.

                    ATTILA
          It's a combination of things. Most
          popular is the cabinetry which we
          do ourselves, custom-to-order. The
          lamps too. Some pieces we've found
          and restored. Audrey does the
          displays.

LÁSZLÓ nods, still visibly moved by the news of his wife. Not betraying much enthusiasm, he turns to AUDREY.

                    LÁSZLÓ
          He speaks like an American from the
          television now-

                    AUDREY
               (demure, posh, defiant)
          Well, we don't have a television
          but he's been here *since before I
          was* born and still doesn't sound
          like any American *I've* ever met.

                    ATTILA
          Eight years ago, we tried opening
          something similar in Manhattan but
          we lasted just two months.

                    AUDREY
          We couldn't compete with the name
          brands.

                    ATTILA
          Newlyweds come in with an issue of
          Better Homes and Gardens and say,
          "We'd like that table next to the
          perfume ad."

He exhales demonstratively.

                    ATTILA (CONT'D)
          We'd say to them, "*well, we can
          make you something like that.*" And
          they say, "*no sir, we want exactly
          that!*" Turns out that we don't like
          New York at all. No charm, right
          Audrey?

She nods.

                    ATTILA (CONT'D)
          Every little urchin you come across
          - seller, buyer, delivery boy - is
          running a hustle.

ATTILA arrives at a door at the back, and sorts through a ring of keys without looking at LÁSZLÓ.

                    AUDREY
          I'm from Connecticut myself. Do you
          know it?

Before LÁSZLÓ can respond...

                    ATTILA
          Audrey, of course he doesn't know
          it. He just got here.

ATTILA opens the door and flips on a light. The bedroom set-up is makeshift and austere.

                    ATTILA (CONT'D)
          I cleared out some space for you in
          the back. Audrey made you a bed.
          There's just the cot and the lamp
          for now but feel free to take
          anything you want from the
          showroom.

                    LÁSZLÓ
          That's all I need.

Anxious and embarrassed, ATTILA continues on yammering.

                    ATTILA
          For the employee restroom, you just
          exit the front door, and walk
          around back where I parked the car.
          There's a staircase there, it takes
          you up to our apartment. If you
          need anything just knock.

The three of them don't bother stepping inside so ATTILA shuts the door and leads them around the shop's interior perimeter.

> AUDREY
> You know, we know somebody, who can take a look at your nose.

> LÁSZLÓ
> I thought- maybe no one would notice.

LÁSZLÓ smiles a little, having tried to make a joke with almost no inflection.

> AUDREY
> What happened, if you don't mind my asking?

ATTILA shoots her a look. LÁSZLÓ struggles a bit with the language speaking slowly, methodically.

> LÁSZLÓ
> (anecdotal)
> I jumped from a rail car. A few moments later there was a loud cracking sound so I thought I had been shot in the head- but I had *merely* run into the branch of a tree. No one was running after me.

AUDREY and ATTILA aren't sure how to respond.

> LÁSZLÓ (CONT'D)
> I take something for the pain but I would like to have it looked at. Thank you.

> AUDREY
> I'll give Kenneth a call.

ATTILA puts his arm around LÁSZLÓ and guides him away from AUDREY to an office area in the showroom's back corner.

> ATTILA
> Come and take a seat at my desk.

ATTILA takes the boss' chair. LÁSZLÓ sits across from him like it's a job interview.

> ATTILA (CONT'D)
> Is it smaller than you expected?

> LÁSZLÓ
> What?

> ATTILA
> The shop.

> LÁSZLÓ
> No, not at all. I had no expectation.

LÁSZLÓ analyzes ATTILA's business cards which read: **MILLER & SONS**.

LÁSZLÓ (CONT'D)
Who is Miller?

ATTILA
I am Miller.

LÁSZLÓ
You are Molnár.

ATTILA
Not anymore.

LÁSZLÓ
No Miller, No Sons.

ATTILA
(shrugs)
Folks here like a family business-

ATTILA offers LÁSZLÓ a cigarette.

ATTILA (CONT'D)
So, what do you think?

LÁSZLÓ
Of the furniture?

ATTILA
Well, I meant of everything so far - Philadelphia - but sure the pieces on the floor also...

LÁSZLÓ
(blunt)
They are not so beautiful.

ATTILA looks a little hurt but saves face.

ATTILA
That's what you're here for, Maestro.

ATTILA lights his cigarette.

ATTILA (CONT'D)
Next month, I can put you on the payroll. You're welcome to eat with us upstairs on Sundays.

LÁSZLÓ
You and your wife have done quite enough.

ATTILA
Don't mention it.

LÁSZLÓ
No, I do *mention*- thank you, Attila.

LÁSZLÓ motions to AUDREY.

> LÁSZLÓ (CONT'D)
> (Yiddish)
> *Gentile? (Goy?)*

ATTILA nods.

> ATTILA
> She's Catholic.

Corrects himself.

> ATTILA (CONT'D)
> *We* are Catholic.

15 **INT. FURNITURE SHOWROOM - BACKROOM - NIGHT** 15

CLOSE ON -

Under the glow of lamp light, ERZSÉBET's letter in Hungarian reads...

László, I am alive. Attila tells me that you, too, are alive and en route to him from Bremerhaven. Rejoice! I cried out in ecstasy to have news of you...

The note trembles in LÁSZLÓ's withering hands. Off-screen, he can be heard again weeping. He strokes the text lovingly and murmurs its text to himself. He sets the note down and begins sketching the first lines of an architectural drawing.

> LÁSZLÓ
> (murmurs)
> *Erzsébet...*

CUE: Solo piano concludes.

FADE TO BLACK.

16 **EXT. OLD CITY CHURCH SOUP KITCHEN - MORNING** 16

A new season has arrived. Pigeons are everywhere and rain drizzles down on a long queue of impoverished families waiting on line for food. We pan across to LÁSZLÓ who stands solo amongst the families in line. **His nose has healed somewhat.**

A man in uniform stands ahead of LÁSZLÓ playing "*I Spy*" with his little boy. He will come to be known later as **GORDON**.

> GORDON
> It's your turn now, William.

The boy, **WILLIAM**, has his eyes locked on LÁSZLÓ.

> WILLIAM
> I spy- with my eye- something- blue.

GORDON turns around and regards LÁSZLÓ.

>   GORDON
>   Is it this gentleman's coat?

>   LÁSZLÓ
>   He is clever- there is some blue in
>   it.

LÁSZLÓ grins in acknowledgement. A volunteer shouts out...

>   VOLUNTEER (O.S.)
>   Kitchen's closed, folks! Get back
>   early tomorrow.

The crowd hollers with disappointment.

>   GORDON
>   Wait, hold on! I got a kid here!

The disgruntled VOLUNTEER shouts back.

>   VOLUNTEER
>   We're fresh out! Come see me early
>   tomorrow and I'll make sure he gets
>   a plate.

LÁSZLÓ joins in.

>   LÁSZLÓ
>   (shouts)
>   You must have a slice of bread-
>   he's only a little boy!

>   VOLUNTEER
>   How many more times do you all want
>   me to say it?! There's nothing left
>   here!

GORDON regards LÁSZLÓ.

>   GORDON
>   Thank you-

>   LÁSZLÓ
>   Will he be all right-?

>   GORDON
>   There's somewhere else we can try
>   tonight.

>   LÁSZLÓ
>   Let him sleep tomorrow. I can be
>   here early to- hold a place.

17   **INT. ABOVE GROUND TROLLEY - LATER**   17

LÁSZLÓ holds a leather strap for balance in a packed tram car. He regards a woman's purse in front of him. After a moment, she exits.

LÁSZLÓ shifts around as a new group of pedestrians come aboard. Two well-dressed businessmen enter and stand to his left. The train begins to move. With each sharp turn, the passengers lean with the train.

LÁSZLÓ's left hand enters the business man's coat pocket but quickly recedes with nothing in its grasp. His expression is grave, debased. He makes a decision and slowly re-positions himself to the other side of the two men.

> LÁSZLÓ
> Excuse me.

He waits for the tram to make another sharp turn, and as it does....

LÁSZLÓ's right hand enters the businessman's coat pocket. He quickly pulls it back with something in his grip.

LÁSZLÓ hesitates to look down and see the fruit of his labor.

CLOSE ON -

He opens his hand to reveal a soiled tissue.

18 **INT. THE CONGREGATION MIKVEH ISRAEL - LATER** 18

LÁSZLÓ sits for a service, a kippah atop his crown.

> CHAZZAN (O.S.)
> (Hebrew)
> *We will hallow and adore You as the sweet words of the assembly of the holy Seraphim who thrice repeat "holy" unto You, as it is written by Your prophet: And they call one to another and Say...*

> LÁSZLÓ
> (Hebrew)
> *Holy, holy, holy is the L-rd of hosts; the whole earth is full of His glory.*

19 **INT. THE CONGREGATION MIKVEH ISRAEL - LATER** 19

LONG LENS ON -

LÁSZLÓ approaches **RABBI ZUNZ** in a greeting processional.

> LÁSZLÓ
> *Boker tov.* Rabbi Zunz-?

> RABBI ZUNZ
> Yes?

                    LÁSZLÓ
               (discreet)
          My niece and wife- I have learned
          the two are stuck at the Austrian
          boundary-

RABBI ZUNZ understands.

                    RABBI ZUNZ
          Wait not many minutes for me and we
          can speak after. Mikveh Israel can
          try and help but from here it is
          very difficult, as you know-

LÁSZLÓ nods graciously and extends a hand in thanks.

20   **INT./ EXT. WORKSHOP/ FOUNDRY - DAY**   20

A SERIES OF ANGLES ON -

LÁSZLÓ's meticulous process as he constructs a chaise lounge and 2 tubular metal Bauhaus style chairs.

- Sparks illuminate LÁSZLÓ's face as he presides over two men welding a few pieces of metal together in a garage. ATTILA assists them.

- LÁSZLÓ feverishly pencils a drawing.

- Pan up an elegant S-shaped plank of soft wood.

- Inside, with the precision of a tailor, LÁSZLÓ measures a strip of leather for the chair back.

- ATTILA pulls the leather down, and the two stand back to observe the object which appears somehow incomplete.

- Pan across other masterful drawings which are carelessly strewn about.

The flow of work and ideas for a wide variety of different objects appears infinite.

21   **EXT. FURNITURE SHOWROOM - LATER**   21

AUDREY observes LÁSZLÓ's two finished chairs and a functional utilitarian shelving unit in the shop front display. She paces back and forth on the sidewalk.

                    AUDREY
          Well, I'm not sure what to do with
          them is all.

She bites her lip.

                    AUDREY (CONT'D)
          What do you think I should pair
          them with?

                    LÁSZLÓ
          Leave it-

                    AUDREY
          How?

                    LÁSZLÓ
          Leave it like that.

AUDREY reaches a conclusion.

                    AUDREY
          They look like tricycles.

LÁSZLÓ looks a little puzzled.

                    LÁSZLÓ
          What's that?

                    AUDREY
          A bike for kids.

22   **EXT. EMPLOYEE RESTROOM - MORNING**   22

     LÁSZLÓ shaves himself with a straight blade. As he does, he
     charmingly practices an embellished American accent in the
     mirror.

                    LÁSZLÓ
               (emphasizing his R's)
          Peter Piper picked a peck of
          pickled peppers. Did Peter Piper
          pick a peck of pickled peppers? If
          Peter Piper picked a peck of
          pickled peppers, where's the peck
          of pickled peppers Peter Piper
          picked?

23   **EXT. FURNITURE SHOWROOM - MOMENTS LATER**   23

     LÁSZLÓ exits the bathroom with a towel around his neck and WE
     TRACK with him down the sidewalk. When he reaches the front
     of the building, as he rounds the corner, he bumps into
     ATTILA who grabs him by the arm.

                    ATTILA
          Get over here.

We follow behind them urgently...

                    ATTILA (CONT'D)
          We have an important customer
          inside; furnished him a two-story
          office space downtown on the cheap
          last year. He's interested in us
          doing some built-in work at a
          residence.

| 24 | **INT. FURNITURE SHOWROOM - MOMENTS LATER** | 24 |

HARRY LEE VAN BUREN, 30s, handsome, smokes in an office chair towards the back of the shop. ATTILA hurries back to his desk. LÁSZLÓ, still holding a razor blade, follows behind him.

>   ATTILA
>   Mr. Van Buren, this is my cousin,
>   László.

LÁSZLÓ nods.

>   HARRY LEE
>   Please - that's what people call my
>   father. Call me Harry.

>   ATTILA
>   (to LÁSZLÓ)
>   *Harry* would like some shelving
>   units installed over at his
>   family's property in Doylestown.

HARRY addresses the blade in LÁSZLÓ's hand.

>   HARRY LEE
>   Sorry to interrupt.

>   HARRY LEE (CONT'D)
>   I hoped someone might follow me out
>   there to take a look at my father's
>   study. My sister and I'd like to
>   surprise him by turning it into a
>   proper library.

>   LÁSZLÓ
>   How do you mean?

>   HARRY LEE
>   -place is in complete disarray; a
>   whole mess of books and paperwork
>   so I guess we'd just like some tall
>   shelves and cabinetry installed?
>   Maybe make him a ladder with little
>   wheels on it, you know, like you'd
>   see in a real library? He's a
>   voracious reader.

>   ATTILA
>   We can make you something like
>   that. Let me have Audrey come down
>   to keep an eye on the place. I'll
>   pull the van around.

>   HARRY LEE
>   Fantastic.

| 25 | **EXT. COUNTY ROADS - LATER** | 25 |

ULTRA-WIDE LOW ANGLE ON -

Asphalt rushes at us. The road bends and curves.

26   **EXT. ATTILA'S BEDFORD VAN - CONTINUOUS**   26

In the front windshield's reflection we view HARRY LEE's sports car as it speeds with thrilling abandon down the local county roads.

>   ATTILA
> They've got something like nine hundred acres out here, I'm not kidding. A few buildings downtown too- one of them's a department store.

>   LÁSZLÓ
> They pay you well?

>   ATTILA
> On the last job, they paid okay. They took on a lot of pieces though. Kept adding to the order. Even at a discount, it adds up...

ATTILA references HARRY LEE's sports car.

>   ATTILA (CONT'D)
> His old man got flush adapting production techniques to expedite the manufacturing of cargo ships during the war.

ATTILA struggles to keep up in his van.

>   ATTILA (CONT'D)
>   (shouting at the window)
> Christ, is this guy trying to shake us? Does he think he's in a drag race? Come on, already!

27   **EXT. VAN BUREN GATES - LATER**   27

HARRY LEE opens a gate and waves them past.

>   HARRY LEE
>   (shouts)
> Stay left until you see the main house. You can park wherever you'd like.

ATTILA turns his clumsy green Bedford through the front gates.

28   **EXT. VAN BUREN ESTATE - MOMENTS LATER**   28

ANGLE ON -

The view of the striking estate framed by a tree-lined driveway.

CUE: The score is ominous and it hums.

29   **INT. VAN BUREN ESTATE - FOYER - MOMENTS LATER**   29

We are tight on LÁSZLÓ as he moves through the house. He's led by his cousin and HARRY LEE. **LÁSZLÓ takes note of various modernist sculptures on pedestals around the entryway.**

> HARRY LEE
> I do appreciate you coming out here on such short notice, gentlemen. Father's away only until next Friday so I was anxious to pin this down.

> ATTILA
> It's no inconvenience for us, chief.

They turn a corner and ATTILA shoots a glance at LÁSZLÓ.

> ATTILA (CONT'D)
> It's your lucky day too cause my cousin here is a licensed architect, and a specialist in renovations... He's even designed a library before, back at home. I mean, a whole city library.

> HARRY LEE
> What city is that?

LÁSZLÓ speaks...

> LÁSZLÓ
> Budapest.

> HARRY LEE
> (cheerful)
> I see. Never been.

30   **INT. VAN BUREN'S STUDY - MOMENTS LATER**   30

HARRY LEE pushes a door open to reveal a dark, octagonal-shaped study framed by heavy curtains drawn to cover the floor-to-ceiling windows.

Only a small shaft of light is allowed in through the corbel glass dome above. Hardbound books are stacked on and scattered across Van Buren's desk, floor space, and the existing two meter high bookshelves.

HARRY LEE pulls a curtain aside flooding the room with light. Particulate floats all around him.

> HARRY LEE
> Don't mind the mess.

LÁSZLÓ and ATTILA observe the space.

HARRY LEE (CONT'D)
I'm thinking... Shelves up to the ceiling, and some good reading lamps. Perhaps some wall fixtures that extend? Father always keeps the curtains drawn.

LÁSZLÓ
-to protect the books from the sunlight. We are south-facing here.

HARRY LEE
Sure.

ATTILA
What's your budget?

HARRY LEE
What's your estimate?

LÁSZLÓ
Depends on the materials.

HARRY LEE
Well, make it of reasonable quality. Maybe a nice place for him to sit and read, as well? A good chair or bench for him against the window?

LÁSZLÓ regards the stained-glass dome above. There is an ugly diagonal crack across it.

LÁSZLÓ
Would you like us to replace that?

HARRY LEE
If there's time, why not? A branch fell on it during that nasty storm last summer; a *tropical depression* they called it.

HARRY LEE stops to think, arrives at a number...

HARRY LEE (CONT'D)
Keep it below six or seven hundred dollars, can you? My sister and I are splitting it. I don't want any unexpected add-ons.

ATTILA masks his enthusiasm.

ATTILA
Don't worry, we'll come in on-budget. You want this all done by next Friday, you said?

HARRY LEE
Thursday night, preferably. I can't be here during the week but the staff can let you in, and if anything comes up, have them ring me at the office.

                    LÁSZLÓ
              (firm)
          To be finished on Thursday, we need
          extra hands. Including materials
          and glass, eight hundred dollars.

31   **INT. ATTILA'S APARTMENT - NIGHT**   31

    CUE: Dinah Shore's *Buttons and Bows* plays on the
    gramophone.

    LÁSZLÓ sits at a small kitchen table backed up against the
    wall. The overhead lamp makes a dark shadow across his face.
    He watches ATTILA who is wildly drunk, dancing with his tipsy
    wife, AUDREY. He convincingly mouths the lyrics to "Buttons
    and Bows" which makes AUDREY laugh.

                    ATTILA
          Dance with us! Come on! Cut a rug.

                    LÁSZLÓ
          No, thank you.

    ATTILA pulls open his sweaty collar, grabs an apron, wrapping
    it around his waist like a dress and continues mouthing
    Dinah's lyrics.

                    ATTILA
          Don't be a spoiled-sport!

                    LÁSZLÓ
              (smiles)
          I'm not sure what that is but no
          thank you.

    CUE: The track comes to an end.

                    ATTILA
              (to Audrey)
          Flip it for the other side-

    ATTILA catches his breath.

                    ATTILA (CONT'D)
          You should have seen him talking up
          the price today! I was ready to
          settle at 450.

                    LÁSZLÓ
          I wasn't doing that. I was just
          telling him how much it will cost.

    To AUDREY...

                    ATTILA
          I thought he was about to blow it
          for us!

    To LÁSZLÓ...

                    ATTILA (CONT'D)
          I did! I honestly did! I thought
          you were going to completely blow
          it but *you held your ground*. That's
          what makes you a professional.

LÁSZLÓ appears embarrassed.

                    LÁSZLÓ
          Hopefully, it's not *only* that-

ATTILA turns to AUDREY, playfully turning the screws on her.

                    ATTILA
          You know, László's bride was a goy,
          too, when they met, but *she*
          converted for him-

AUDREY rolls her eyes.

                    AUDREY
          I should put a muzzle on you.

A new track comes on.

                    AUDREY (CONT'D)
          Oh! This is my favorite.

                    ATTILA
          Dance with her, László!

AUDREY looks a little embarrassed.

                    AUDREY
          He doesn't want to.

                    ATTILA
              (drunk and antagonizing)
          Don't keep her waiting, cousin.
          It's her favorite song.

ATTILA's tone has darkened the atmosphere. LÁSZLÓ finally stands and approaches AUDREY.

HANDHELD ON -

LÁSZLÓ takes AUDREY by the waist and they sway back and forth. There's a palpable erotic tension.

                    AUDREY
          You're awfully skinny, aren't you?

LÁSZLÓ nods, still swaying rhythmically.

                    ATTILA
          See! It's like riding a bike.

ATTILA wraps his arms around them both and the three sway and sway.

AUDREY longs for LÁSZLÓ.

32 **INT. ATTILA'S APARTMENT - LATER** 32

ATTILA's passed out on the bed.

The bathroom door is open. LÁSZLÓ is hunched over the bathtub pissing into it. He sweats profusely.

A NEW ANGLE reveals AUDREY smoking a cigarette watching him.

> AUDREY
> (deadpan)
> You missed the toilet.

LÁSZLÓ finishes and stumbles out.

> LÁSZLÓ
> What-

> AUDREY
> (murmurs)
> Better than the carpet, I suppose.

BEAT.

> AUDREY (CONT'D)
> When do you expect your wife might join you, Mr. Toth-? There isn't room for two in that storage space, I'll tell you.

> LÁSZLÓ
> I wish I knew, Audrey. Thank you for the dinner.

An awkward beat passes between them.

> AUDREY
> Attila's shown me some magazine pictures of the projects you did at your firm. You're not what I expected from what I read about you.

He leans against the door frame, practically trying to crawl out.

> LÁSZLÓ
> *I'm* not what *I* expected-

> AUDREY
> I'm sure you could get a job, a better job, at a firm here.

> LÁSZLÓ
> I then-

He breathes.

                  LÁSZLÓ (CONT'D)
      -would be working- *for someone.*

                  AUDREY
      Better than sleeping in a storage
      closet.

LONG BEAT. LÁSZLÓ understands.

                  LÁSZLÓ
      I'll look for somewhere else to
      stay. Thank you again for the
      dinner.

LÁSZLÓ opens the door and exits.

33   **INT. VAN BUREN'S STUDY - DAY**   33

ATTILA and LÁSZLÓ remove the existing Art Deco shelving units from their place.

34   **EXT. VAN BUREN ESTATE - DUSK**   34

Next to a two meter tall pile of debris, ATTILA and LÁSZLÓ craft new units for installation.

35   **INT. VAN BUREN'S STUDY - EVENING**   35

A SERIES OF ANGLES -

The room is empty. The walls are stripped. The curtains are gone. Alone, LÁSZLÓ sweeps the floor clean with a broom. He stops at the center and regards the space.

36   **INT. VAN BUREN'S STUDY - NEW DAY**   36

BIRDS-EYE VIEW ON-

LÁSZLÓ stands at the center of the room. He is surrounded by a few **HIRED MEN** (one is recognizable from the Old City Church Soup Kitchen, **GORDON**). Each of them are supporting a large plywood plate.

                  LÁSZLÓ
      One - two - three!

The men simultaneously lift the plates, standing them up to completely enclose the room in an octagonal shape. At the central point of action, it mimics a flower blooming.

The windows now sealed in darkness, save for the sole shaft of light let through the stained-glass dome above.

CLOSE ON -

The rouge tinted light illuminates LÁSZLÓ's expression as he gazes up at it.

37 **INT. VAN BUREN'S STUDY - NEW DAY** 37

LÁSZLÓ speaks to GORDON and ATTILA.

>   LÁSZLÓ
>   Set each panel to 45°.

GORDON mimics LÁSZLÓ's instruction.

>   GORDON
>   Like this?
>
>   LÁSZLÓ
>   Yes, that's right. That looks
>   right, doesn't it? The books shall
>   fan outwards, you see?

LÁSZLÓ demonstrates with his hands passionately.

>   LÁSZLÓ (CONT'D)
>   *Like so.*
>
>   ATTILA
>   All in the same direction?
>
>   LÁSZLÓ
>   The long panels, yes. The shelves
>   themselves, however, can vary in
>   height to accommodate the larger
>   volumes our client had been
>   stacking on the floor.

38 **EXT. VAN BUREN ESTATE ROOF - DAY** 38

HANDHELD ON -

LÁSZLÓ, ATTILA, GORDON, and the other hired hands work on the Victorian gabled roof above Van Buren's study. Amongst a cobweb of ropes and a makeshift pulley system, the men pull the rope taut, painstakingly lifting the detached glass dome from the roof of the study with a short crane arm.

LÁSZLÓ directs GORDON who, in turn, directs the rest of the group.

>   LÁSZLÓ
>   Slowly, Gordon. One steady
>   movement.
>
>   GORDON
>   (shouts)
>   *Slowly, boys!*

The men operate the pulley system successfully lifting the dome head from its place.

                    LÁSZLÓ
                 (mutters)
            Left, Gordon. Left. And steady.

                    GORDON
                 (shouts)
            All right, good! Now left. (Beat)
            To the left!

One man manually pushes the base of the crane arm employing excessive strength, and **it suddenly swings out too fast, hovering over the driveway.**

                    GROUP
            Hey, christ, watch out!

The group overcorrect the crane's movement causing the dome frame to swing back, gaining velocity, in their direction. The dome hits the corner gutter hard, knocking out one large panel from its frame.

ANGLE ON -

It shatters in the driveway below.

BACK TO -

                    LÁSZLÓ
            No!

LÁSZLÓ scrambles across the shingled roof towards the dome which is stuck at an awkward tilt on the southeast corner of the mansion.

                    GORDON
                 (shouts)
            I said to be careful, goddammit!

                    LÁSZLÓ
                 (shouts re: crane arm)
            Get a hold of that thing!

The group is frozen, spooked. ATTILA calls out...

                    ATTILA
            Everyone all right down there?

                    HIRED MAN
                 (defensive)
            -the glass was already broken.

ANGLE ON -

LÁSZLÓ crawls on all fours to the very edge of the roof where the dome frame is stuck.

                    ATTILA
                 (shouts)
            CAREFUL, LÁSZLÓ!

LÁSZLÓ tries to dislodge the heavy dome frame which grinds against the guttering.

LÁSZLÓ begins to kick at it over and over again. Its an increasingly reckless gesture. Finally, after three kicks, he successfully dislodges the dome from the gutter which causes it to CRASH to the ground. He breathes heavy-

                    LÁSZLÓ
          We have a piece of gutter to
          replace now, as well!

39   **INT. VAN BUREN'S STUDY - DAY**   39

        STRAIGHT UP ON -

        The men outside replace the stained-glass with a flat, clear circular disk. The image recalls a solar eclipse.

        BIRDS-EYE VIEW -

        An intense spherical shaft of light illuminates the center of the room. The bookshelves are now complete, remarkable for their geometry. There is no furniture in the room apart from a visually-arresting chaise lounge which LÁSZLÓ pushes into the very midpoint of sunlight.

40   **INT. VAN BUREN'S STUDY - DUSK**   40

        LÁSZLÓ and ATTILA pull protective linens from the painted wall of shelves. Half the room is now filled with Van Buren's collection of precious tomes. Several modern lamps on scissored extenders poke out in various directions.

41   **EXT. VAN BUREN ESTATE - SAME TIME**   41

        GORDON picks up fragments of stained-glass from the driveway. The massive dome frame is plunked down beside him.

        After some time, the headlights of an automobile blind GORDON from off-screen as he looks up...

42   **INT. VAN BUREN'S STUDY - MOMENTS LATER**   42

        The esteemed and handsome, **HARRISON LEE VAN BUREN SR.**, enters the room in a miserly fury. ATTILA and LÁSZLÓ stand frozen, initially dumbfounded by the intrusion.

                    VAN BUREN
          What's this? What is all this? Who
          has authorized you to come into my
          home and tear everything apart?

        ATTILA blinks.

                    VAN BUREN (CONT'D)
          Who the hell are you?

                    ATTILA
          Uh... Excuse us, sir. This was all
          supposed to be a surprise.
                         (MORE)

ATTILA (CONT'D)
Your son, Harry, told us not to expect you until tomorrow-

VAN BUREN
(shouting)
It is a Goddamned surprise! My mother, an ailing woman, is sitting outside on the driveway too frightened to come inside!

ATTILA
We are sorry to have frightened her.

VAN BUREN
-we brought her here for some *peace and respite* only to discover a strange Negro man roaming around our property.

ATTILA
Sir, your son asked us here to redo your study into a library.

VAN BUREN
A library?

VAN BUREN looks around.

VAN BUREN (CONT'D)
The room- it's *gutted*.

ATTILA
We were just putting everything back in its place.

VAN BUREN
You've turned it all inside out. How the hell do you know its proper place?

LÁSZLÓ finally interjects...

LÁSZLÓ
We have taken excellent care of your things, Mr. Van Buren.

VAN BUREN turns to LÁSZLÓ with a daring expression, provoked by his calm.

VAN BUREN
And who the hell are you?

LÁSZLÓ
László Toth-

ATTILA
László is a licensed architect. He supervised the renovation. And I- I've done business with your son before. I have a furniture shop, *Miller and Son's,* down in Kensington.

VAN BUREN stares, fixated on LÁSZLÓ. The two have an immediate, adversarial connection.

> LÁSZLÓ
> May I show you around the space, sir? Our work lamps aren't doing the work we've done here any justice.

> VAN BUREN
> Your Negro is waiting for you outside the gates so I suggest you pack your things up and leave. I'll confirm all this with my son in the morning. My mother is sick! She needs to be let inside to sleep.

> LÁSZLÓ
> We are finished. That's quite all right.

CUE: A low rumble overtakes the soundtrack.

> CROSS DISSOLVE:

43 **INT. FURNITURE SHOWROOM - BACKROOM - MORNING** 43

LÁSZLÓ snores in a deep sleep, physically exhausted. After a few moments, ATTILA shakes LÁSZLÓ awake.

> ATTILA
> Wake up.

LÁSZLÓ jolts up in fearful defense, but quickly re-gathers himself.

> ATTILA (CONT'D)
> That's a hell of a way to greet the day.

ATTILA lights a cigarette on the edge of his cot.

> ATTILA (CONT'D)
> Harry Lee called.

LÁSZLÓ sits up against the wall, trying to maintain some dignity though caught off-guard.

> ATTILA (CONT'D)
> He says he won't pay.

> LÁSZLÓ
> For the materials?

> ATTILA
> (calm)
> He says we damaged the property and I'm lucky if he doesn't take me to court.

LÁSZLÓ doesn't respond. ATTILA remains calm but his voice quivers with emotion.

              ATTILA (CONT'D)
You've got nothing to say to that? What are you going to do about it?

ATTILA speaks for a moment in Hungarian.

              ATTILA (CONT'D)
        (Hungarian)
I take you into my home. Into my place of business, László, and this is how you thank me?

LÁSZLÓ is again silent.

              ATTILA (CONT'D)
You run my clients out the door? You make a pass at my wife? She told me! *Of course, she told me.* What did you expect?

Silence.

              ATTILA (CONT'D)
Hell, *what did I expect*? You couldn't keep your hands to yourself even when we were kids. Listen up, I won't tell Erzsi this time. I know you've been through a lot. That's what I told Audrey, too. I'm not going to hurt you, but I can't help you anymore either, got it?

LÁSZLÓ breathes, defiant.

                            FADE TO BLACK.

44   **EXT. OLD CITY CHURCH - MORNING**   44

Winter has come again. The bell tolls. HOLD, HOLD...

              LÁSZLÓ (V.O.)
        (in HUNGARIAN)
ERZSÉBET,
I CAN BE REACHED BY MAIL AT A NEW ADDRESS... I WAIT FOR YOU. I WAIT AND WAIT. DO YOU NEED MONEY? WHAT DO YOU NEED?
YOURS, LÁSZLÓ.

45   **INT. OLD CITY CHURCH - SAME**   45

HOMELESS MEN sweep the floor of the shelter.

46 **INT. OLD CITY CHURCH BASEMENT - SAME** 46

The muffled ring of the bell... Homeless families in bunks begin to rise from their beds.

ANGLE ON -

LÁSZLÓ wakes in a bunk clutching a duffle bag that contains his few possessions. **His beard has grown out.**

ANGLE ON -

GORDON and his son sleep through the ruckus in the bunk across from LÁSZLÓ.

>   LÁSZLÓ
>   Gordon-

GORDON stirs awake.

47 **INT. OLD CITY CHURCH BASEMENT - MOMENTS LATER** 47

GORDON is now dressed in functional garments for the day's work. He gently tries to wake his little boy who wants to sleep some more.

>   GORDON
>   (whispers)
>   We got to go. I let you sleep in.
>   Time to get up.

A NUN approaches GORDON.

>   NUN
>   Has Mr. Toth already gone? I'd like
>   a word.

48 **INT. OLD CITY CHURCH BASEMENT LAVATORIES - MOMENTS LATER** 48

STEADICAM ON -

GORDON moves down the hallway and shoulders open the bathroom door.

>   GORDON
>   László!

The door opens to reveal LÁSZLÓ fiddling to stuff a syringe and some barbiturate powder back in its pouch.

>   LÁSZLÓ
>   It's for my injury.

GORDON blinks.

>   GORDON
>   Sister Elizabeth is asking for you.

                    LÁSZLÓ
               I will be right there.

GORDON nods to the junk.

                    GORDON
               Do me a favor and hold off on that
               until we punch out.

49   **EXT. CONSTRUCTION SITE - MORNING**   49

On a second-story high beam, LÁSZLÓ spots GORDON, pulling his
safety leash taut as GORDON leans to wrench several bolts
below frame. GORDON laughs wildly...

                    LÁSZLÓ
               She asked me for my- participation.

                    GORDON
               Like what? They want you to help
               out-

                    LÁSZLÓ
               I already help- *out*. She wants me
               to attend the service on Sundays;
               collect donations.

GORDON looks back at him, takes a break.

                    GORDON
               And what did you say to her?

                    LÁSZLÓ
               I said that I would think about it.

                    GORDON
               That seems fair, no?

LÁSZLÓ shrugs.

                    LÁSZLÓ
               I go to- somewhere else.

GORDON leans down again.

                    GORDON
               Why not ask for a place to stay
               wherever it is that you *do* go!?

                    LÁSZLÓ
               I do not permit my people from home
               to see me as a beggar. Never.

GORDON playfully sings, in retort.

                    GORDON
               (sings)
          *A rose must remain with the sun and
          the rain Or its lovely promise
          won't come true*
          To Each His Own, To Each His Own
          And my own is you-

CUE: To Each His Own by Eddy Howard overtakes the soundtrack.

LÁSZLÓ laughs.

                    GORDON (CONT'D)
               Give me a few inches.

LÁSZLÓ cautiously releases six inches of rope. As he does, he notices an conspicuous black Cadillac Towncar approaching the yard.

50   **EXT. CONSTRUCTION SITE - MOMENTS LATER**   50

LÁSZLÓ shovels aggregate into a cement mixer. GORDON enters from off-screen.

                    GORDON
               (casual)
          There's a son of a bitch here to
          see you.

LÁSZLÓ furrows his brow and looks beyond GORDON to see HARRISON VAN BUREN SR. on approach from some distance.

                    VAN BUREN
          László Toth! Is that you?!

VAN BUREN appears overjoyed, ecstatic. LÁSZLÓ courteously stands to receive him, stoic.

                    VAN BUREN (CONT'D)
          I've been looking for *you*!

LÁSZLÓ shares a dubious glance with GORDON.

                    VAN BUREN (CONT'D)
          No wonder you couldn't be found!
          You've grown a beard!

LÁSZLÓ blinks.

                    LÁSZLÓ
          What can I do for you, sir?

VAN BUREN catches his breath in the cold.

                    VAN BUREN
          I'd like to take *you* for lunch.

                    LÁSZLÓ
          We don't break for another 2 hours.

VAN BUREN
Point out your manager. Let me
educate him.

51   INT. DINER - AFTERNOON   51

A waitress pours coffee for the two of them and exits. VAN BUREN pulls out an edition of **LOOK Magazine** placing it in front of LÁSZLÓ.

VAN BUREN
Have you seen that?

LÁSZLÓ squints, shakes his head.

VAN BUREN (CONT'D)
Well, I can assure you that
everyone else has... Flip to page
19.

LÁSZLÓ handles the magazine like a foreign object.

VAN BUREN (CONT'D)
Where did you study?

LÁSZLÓ
(mutters)
Bauhaus in Dessau.

VAN BUREN
Bauhaus! How marvelous.

ULTRA-CLOSE ON -

A two-page spread on "**HARRISON LEE VAN BUREN - THE FORWARD-THINKER.**"

The large black and white photograph depicts VAN BUREN seated in LÁSZLÓ's chaise lounge illuminated by the spherical window above him.

A second smaller image depicts VAN BUREN standing against the unusual, conceptual shelving units; books fan out around him.

VAN BUREN (O.S.) (CONT'D)
Read the caption below the
photographs.

The caption reads: "*Here, Mr. Van Buren is pictured in his striking, modern at-home-library; entirely suitable for the forward-thinking man.*"

CAMERA PANS TO NEXT BLOCK OF TEXT -

"*He established the Van Buren Shipyards, which built Liberty ships during World War II, after which he formed Van Buren Aluminum and Van Buren Steel.*

Van Buren is involved in various large-scale construction projects such as civic centers and dams, and is invested in real estate around the globe."

BACK TO -

VAN BUREN who sips his coffee.

>   VAN BUREN (CONT'D)
> So, what do you think?

>   LÁSZLÓ
> Looks good.

>   VAN BUREN
> Damn right, it does! Why didn't you defend yourself when I came after *you all* like a bat out of hell? I am ashamed of my behavior! I called that American cousin of yours-

Corrects him.

>   LÁSZLÓ
> Attila.

>   VAN BUREN
> Yes, that's right. First, I apologized then *lauded him* with praise, however, he quite honorably redirected me *to you!*

VAN BUREN wags a finger at LÁSZLÓ.

>   VAN BUREN (CONT'D)
> I've since done my homework...

VAN BUREN pulls out an open folder and places it in front of LÁSZLÓ.

>   VAN BUREN (CONT'D)
> These are yours, yes?

LÁSZLÓ leafs through the images in the folder and nods.

>   LÁSZLÓ
> Yes.

>   VAN BUREN
> All of them?

>   LÁSZLÓ
> Yes.

LÁSZLÓ begins to tear up, emotional.

>   VAN BUREN
> I'm sorry, have I upset you?

>   LÁSZLÓ
> No. May I keep these?

>   VAN BUREN
> Of course you may.

LÁSZLÓ
I didn't realize these images were still available, much less of any consequence...

VAN BUREN
They are very artistic.

LÁSZLÓ
Better in the real life.

VAN BUREN
You could have elaborated a bit more on your background! You didn't do yourself any favors back there.

LÁSZLÓ
It was difficult to interject amidst all the shouting-

VAN BUREN smiles.

VAN BUREN
I am ashamed. Really, I am. I acted a fool. My mother was dying - and it's not an excuse - but she died that very weekend at the house.

LÁSZLÓ
I am sorry to hear-

VAN BUREN
Tell me - why is an accomplished foreign architect working construction in Philadelphia of all places? What is that you're working on anyway? *A bowling alley?!*

LÁSZLÓ chooses his words carefully.

LÁSZLÓ
The Reich- rejected myself and my colleagues for our type of work for it was deemed not *Germanic in-character*.

LÁSZLÓ exhales, gravely.

LÁSZLÓ (CONT'D)
I don't wish to be rude but I only have time for the coffee. You were unprepared for what you saw. That is understandable. I am glad you've come to appreciate it.

VAN BUREN
I don't just appreciate it Mr. Toth; I cherish it.

VAN BUREN ignores LÁSZLÓ's wish to leave.

VAN BUREN (CONT'D)
(waxes)
I hate surprises. My *fatheaded* son should have known better, but listen, I haven't come here to boast or to grieve, I've come to pay you the monies you are owed.

VAN BUREN hands him an envelope for dramatic effect.

VAN BUREN (CONT'D)
For what it's worth, it was not my suggestion that you and partners should not be paid. I only found out about all that after the fact.

LÁSZLÓ
We damaged some guttering which we planned to replace. There was a misunderstanding.

VAN BUREN
Enough of that. Take the money.

LÁSZLÓ
(nods)
Thank you.

VAN BUREN
I'd stash that in your undergarments or inside of a shoe.

LÁSZLÓ takes the envelope and starts to slide out of the booth but VAN BUREN takes his hand.

VAN BUREN (CONT'D)
I'd like you to come and see it... In the daylight.

LÁSZLÓ
I've seen it.

VAN BUREN
I'd like you to come and enjoy it, rather.

LÁSZLÓ
All right.

VAN BUREN
Wonderful. I can send a car for you on Sunday morning if you aren't too busy. Write me down your address?

LÁSZLÓ writes it down.

VAN BUREN (CONT'D)
I've found our conversation persuasive and intellectually stimulating.

LÁSZLÓ looks at him, incredulous.

52	**INT. JAZZ BAR - NIGHT**	52

ULTRA-BOWED LENS ON-

GORDON and LÁSZLÓ cheer on a raucous set. Their features are wild and exaggerated like a George Grosz drawing.

53	**INT. JAZZ BAR BATHROOM - LATER**	53

SFX: Someone pounds on the door outside.

BIRD'S-EYE VIEW ON -

LÁSZLÓ and GORDON prep a spoon and dropper.

> LÁSZLÓ
> (shouts)
> -going to be some minutes!

LÁSZLÓ, already very intoxicated...

> LÁSZLÓ (CONT'D)
> Have we been in here long?

> GORDON
> They can wait...

GORDON puts a leather pouch in his mouth and lets it unroll to his chest.

> GORDON (CONT'D)
> (through gritted teeth)
> *Pull that out.*

LÁSZLÓ pulls out an antiquated looking syringe.

> LÁSZLÓ
> Jesus, Gordon.

The coconspirators laugh, having a great time. GORDON spits the pouch from his mouth and LÁSZLÓ extends the spoon to GORDON.

54	**INT. JAZZ BAR - LATER**	54

CUE: The live music plays in ultra slow-motion.

LONG LENS ON -

The two of them are now accompanied by some attractive looking strangers. A woman kisses at LÁSZLÓ's neck but he tries to focus on the music.

WE PAN DOWN to see GORDON blatantly fingering his new girlfriend who sits on a bar stool.

                    BAR MANAGER (O.S.)
                (shouting)
            HEY! HEY! GET THE HELL OUT OF HERE!

LÁSZLÓ and GORDON are slow to respond.

                    BAR MANAGER (CONT'D)
                (shouting)
            Get the hell out or I'll beat the
            shit out of you two.

LÁSZLÓ comically vomits on himself where he stands.

                    BAR MANAGER (CONT'D)
            OH, HOLY HELL. I'm gonna kill that
            son of a bitch!

55   **EXT. JAZZ BAR - MOMENTS LATER**   55

The BAR MANAGER and a bouncer beat the hell out of LÁSZLÓ who laughs madly. STEAM RISES from the sewer grates.

ANGLE ON -

The *crack* of LÁSZLÓ's nose re-breaking.

                    LÁSZLÓ
            My nose! Damn it.

56   **EXT. OLD CITY CHURCH - MORNING**   56

LÁSZLÓ exits, his face battered and nose swollen. He lights a cigarette then after a beat, notices VAN BUREN's Town Car parked on the corner with the motor running.

57   **INT. AUTOMOBILE - LATER**   57

CLOSE ON -

LÁSZLÓ sits in the backseat of the Towncar taking in the fresh country air through an open window. He tries to pull himself together.

                    DRIVER (O.S.)
            There's a pressed shirt and jacket
            hanging to your left, Mr. Toth.

58   **INT. VAN BUREN ESTATE DINING ROOM - LATER**   58

A Christmas party is in full-swing. LÁSZLÓ is shown into a dining area where a group of thirty aristocrats have gathered for pre-luncheon cocktails by one end of the table.

                    VAN BUREN
            Ah! There you are! The man of the
            hour!

LÁSZLÓ's smashed face peers out of an oversized penguin suit.
VAN BUREN approaches him, concerned.

                VAN BUREN (CONT'D)
            (hushed)
      What's happened to your face?

                LÁSZLÓ
      Fell off a beam.

VAN BUREN's son, HARRY LEE, comes up behind his father.

                HARRY LEE
      Everyone's famished.

                VAN BUREN
      Harry, you remember each other,
      don't you?

                HARRY LEE
      I do, yes. Good afternoon.

LÁSZLÓ nods. HARRY LEE's sister, **MAGGIE LEE,** comes up behind her brother.

                MAGGIE LEE
      Daddy, the kitchen's asking if we
      could please go ahead and take our
      seats.

                VAN BUREN
      This is Harry's twin sister,
      Maggie.

                MAGGIE LEE
      Hello, Mr. Toth. We love the
      library.

                LÁSZLÓ
      Thank you.

                VAN BUREN
            (to the crowd)
      All right, everyone, let's eat.

59   **INT. VAN BUREN ESTATE DINING ROOM - LATER**   59

LÁSZLÓ, who looks a mess, sits in a corner chair between a middle-aged couple, **MICHAEL** and **MICHELLE HOFFMAN,** and VAN BUREN who now sits at the head of the table. VAN BUREN brags...

                VAN BUREN
      He won't tout his own
      accomplishments but Mr. Toth's work
      is celebrated throughout much of
      Western and Central Europe. There
      have been many features about him
      in the architecture journals if you
      follow that sort of thing.

MICHAEL HOFFMAN
What was your focus?

LÁSZLÓ eats somewhat ravenously.

LÁSZLÓ
Theaters, synagogues- Restorations.
Some, quite unusual.

MICHELLE HOFFMAN
Are you married, Mr. Toth?

LÁSZLÓ stops eating. It pains him to speak of it.

LÁSZLÓ
Yes, but my wife, she- she is still
in Europe.

MICHELLE HOFFMAN
Why is that?

LÁSZLÓ
We were separated. Forcibly.

MICHAEL HOFFMAN
Where is it you come from, if you
don't mind my asking? I can't place
the accent.

LÁSZLÓ
The city of Budapest.

MICHAEL asides, explaining to his wife...

MICHAEL HOFFMAN
Ravaged during the war- just
terrible.

MICHELLE HOFFMAN
Oh my, what was it like, the war?
We hear some stories here that make
one's toes curl.

LÁSZLÓ
I would not know where to begin,
Mrs. Hoffman.

MICHELLE HOFFMAN
Do you plan on returning to Europe?

LÁSZLÓ
She tries to come now, here, to
join me- but the situation is
difficult.

MICHAEL HOFFMAN
With Roosevelt gone now that should
make things easier.

LÁSZLÓ
He is gone, but everyone is still frightened that people like me are a threat to your national defense-

MICHELLE HOFFMAN
When you say 'people,' you mean Jews? We're Jewish.

MICHAEL HOFFMAN
(explains dryly)
Michelle converted.

LÁSZLÓ asides...

LÁSZLÓ
As did my Erzsébet. It required a great deal of commitment and study, and yet, few at home recognized her for it.

LÁSZLÓ japes.

LÁSZLÓ (CONT'D)
A pity the National Socialists couldn't see it their way.

LÁSZLÓ shrugs off the trauma, as he returns to the track of their dinner conversation.

LÁSZLÓ (CONT'D)
But not only Jewish. Foreign people. I was fortunate to depart from Bremerhaven when I did. Truman's order facilitated the transfer of my group. Others were not so lucky.

VAN BUREN finally joins in the conversation.

VAN BUREN
That sounds very painful, László. We are terribly sorry for you. Michael is my friend and attorney- *in that order*.

He turns to MICHAEL.

VAN BUREN (CONT'D)
Michael, is this a process your firm might help to expedite?

MICHAEL turns to LÁSZLÓ.

LÁSZLÓ
I'm afraid that it's not so simple. My wife cannot leave my niece behind because she is young, motherless, and very sick.

                    MICHAEL HOFFMAN
          It's just the two of them? I'd be
          glad to make an inquiry on your
          behalf. You know, there's something
          called The Displaced Persons Act
          that's recently gone into effect.
          It will allow some 200,000 European
          persons admission for permanent
          residence. You can read about it in
          the paper now.

                    VAN BUREN
          He won't boast but Michael's firm
          represents the office of the Vice
          President.

                    LÁSZLÓ
          -president?

                    VAN BUREN
          Of the United States!

                    MICHAEL HOFFMAN
          Come see me in our Philadelphia
          office on Monday.

MICHAEL reaches into his pocket and hands LÁSZLÓ a business card.

                    MICHAEL HOFFMAN (CONT'D)
          Telephone this line, and my
          assistant can arrange. She'll tell
          you what we'll need you both to
          provide.

MICHELLE places her hand on LÁSZLÓ's.

                    MICHELLE HOFFMAN
          Michael can help you.

MICHAEL nods, empathetic.

                    MICHAEL HOFFMAN
                (Hebrew)
          Bevakasha.

A SERVER pours wine in VAN BUREN's glass.

                    VAN BUREN
                (to SERVER)
          We'll take coffee in the study.

60   **INT. FOYER / STUDY - EARLY EVENING**   60

    CUE: The score broods then gives way to an elegiac piano
    theme.

    ULTRA-WIDE ANGLE ON -

    The light is extraordinarily beautiful. It looks like a Saul
    Leiter picture.

The aristocrats all chat amongst themselves sipping coffees and cognac.

NEW ANGLE ON -

LÁSZLÓ and VAN BUREN are deep in-conversation sitting in two chairs the main foyer whiles guests observe the library nearby.

                  VAN BUREN
             (longing, drunk lucidity)
        I was married once and she gave me
        two beautiful children.
        Nevertheless, my mother Margaret
        and the twins demanded my attention-
        every minute of my *scarce* personal
        time. Things became awkward between
        my ex-wife and Margaret so we
        separated amicably...

VAN BUREN lights a cigar. He might be drunk.

                  VAN BUREN (CONT'D)
        Margaret raised me on her own in
        Rochester. Just the two of us. Her
        parents had disowned her for "*a
        child out of wedlock,*" so she was
        my only real family, other than the
        twins later on in life, of
        course...

VAN BUREN speaks rhythmically, hypnotically.

                  VAN BUREN (CONT'D)
        I'll tell you, shortly before they
        died, my mother's parents - *I
        hesitate to call them my
        grandparents* - they reached out to
        Margaret and me after reading an
        article on the reported success of
        my first company.

VAN BUREN asides...

                  VAN BUREN (CONT'D)
        In actual fact, we weren't doing
        all that well at the time and would
        soon shutter our doors, but this
        was not yet public knowledge.

VAN BUREN takes a sip of his drink.

                  VAN BUREN (CONT'D)
        -you might have concluded from our
        prior interactions, I am blunt, not
        hyperbolic or particularly
        sentimental, but my mother was
        defenseless to their chumminess.
        She argued that '*they could very
        well be sick or dying,*" and perhaps
        "*they really needed the money...*" I
        didn't like seeing Margaret, an
        ordinarily pragmatic person,
        reduced to such bromidic
        assumptions but I agreed to meet
        them in-person;
                  (MORE)

VAN BUREN (CONT'D)
in part, to appease her, as well as
to satisfy the curiosities of my
lineage.

A PARTY GUEST comes over and interjects...

PARTY GUEST
It's very clever, isn't it? The way
the space seems to envelop you.

VAN BUREN
I think so, yes.

PARTY GUEST
It reminds me of a short story I
read about a never-ending library,
a labyrinth. Are you working on
anything at present, Mr. Toth?

LÁSZLÓ
A bowling alley.

The PARTY GUEST furrows his brow.

VAN BUREN
Pardon me, but I was just in the
middle of telling our friend a
story.

PARTY GUEST
Oh, not at all. Excuse me.

The PARTY GUEST moves on.

LÁSZLÓ
You agreed to see them?

VAN BUREN nods.

VAN BUREN
We exchanged pleasantries over the
telephone and I offered to visit
them at their modest apartment
residence in a neighboring town.

VAN BUREN asides...

VAN BUREN (CONT'D)
I laughed to realize they'd been *so
nearby* all those years!

Back to the body of the story...

VAN BUREN (CONT'D)
On the drive over, I had time to
think and finally arrived at a
figure I felt comfortable offering
the two of them - seeing that they
were, *whether I liked it or not*,
our only living relatives...
(MORE)

VAN BUREN (CONT'D)
I was received hospitably so I swiftly moved to explain that I had made them out a cheque for the amount of $25,000. When I handed it over, they appeared relieved but perhaps a little disappointed at the figure. They were courteous and thanked me, all the same.

VAN BUREN pauses for effect.

VAN BUREN (CONT'D)
I was quite uncomfortable but before hurrying off I asked them a question; *"what will you do with all that money?"* They rambled on about miracles or some such thing. For a moment, everything in their immediate line of view seemed solvable, *achievable*! They would finally be *all right*. What a thoughtful grandson I was!

VAN BUREN smiles.

VAN BUREN (CONT'D)
Upon departure, *before I had reached the edge of their front lawn*, the two of them ran out after me shouting! - *"You've forgotten your signature, Harrison!"*

VAN BUREN exhales demonstratively.

VAN BUREN (CONT'D)
I summoned the courage to be frank and speak to them as adults. I had not *forgotten*, I said, but was ultimately not *compelled* to sign due to the blunder of their response! *If only* they'd been sick or dying as my mother had previously suggested, how glad I would have been to ease their troubles - but they appeared perfectly healthy to me!

VAN BUREN sighs.

VAN BUREN (CONT'D)
They took it as such a shock that for a moment I thought that *that* might kill them *right there on the front lawn* - but the two just wept and came apart like beggars... It was all much more disturbing than I'd imagined it in my head so on the condition that they let Margaret alone from then on, I struck them a separate cheque for the amount of $500 and signed.

BEAT.

VAN BUREN (CONT'D)
That is how much I loved my mother, Mr. Toth. We did things for each other!

LÁSZLÓ
(deadpan)
What could they expect after the way they had treated you both.

VAN BUREN
Yes, yes, that's exactly how I see it.

LÁSZLÓ blinks.

VAN BUREN (CONT'D)
So, answer me one question; why architecture?

LÁSZLÓ
Is it a test?

VAN BUREN
Not at all.

LÁSZLÓ smiles through the pain of his broken nose.

LÁSZLÓ
(matter-of-fact)
Nothing can be of its own explanation- is there a better description of a cube than that of its construction? You know, some years ago, in March, a stranger knocked at the classroom door of the university where I frequently lectured. At once, all that was familiar and important to us was gone. We were too well-known at home. I thought my reputation might help to protect us but- it was the *opposite*. There was no way to remain anonymous; nowhere for my family to go.

LÁSZLÓ sighs and changes course.

LÁSZLÓ (CONT'D)
There was a war on, and yet it is my understanding that many of the sites of my projects have survived and are still there in the city.

He smiles again and continues, choosing his words carefully.

LÁSZLÓ (CONT'D)
When the terrible recollections of what happened in Europe have ceased to humiliate us, I expect them to serve instead as a political stimulus, sparking the upheavals that so frequently occur in the cycles of peoplehood.
(MORE)

LÁSZLÓ (CONT'D)
          I already anticipate a communal
          rhetoric of anger and fear; a whole
          river of such frivolities may flow
          un-dammed, but my buildings were
          devised to endure such erosion of
          the Danube's shoreline.

VAN BUREN is intoxicated by LÁSZLÓ's response.

                    VAN BUREN
          What a poetic reply! You must have
          been a beloved professor! I've said
          it before but I *do* find our
          conversations intellectually
          stimulating.

WE PAN UP with VAN BUREN as he rises from his chair to address the room.

                    VAN BUREN (CONT'D)
          Everyone, take your brandy and join
          me outside! I have a fantastic
          surprise.

61   **EXT. FOREST TRAIL/ VISTA - TWILIGHT**   61

WIDE ON -

Ghostly silhouettes march across a footbridge near the estate.

                    MICHAEL HOFFMAN
          Where in the hell are you taking
          us, Harrison?! It's freezing out
          here.

                    MICHELLE HOFFMAN
              (laughs)
          Try doing this in heels, Michael!

                    VAN BUREN
          Don't be impatient! It isn't far.

ULTRA-WIDE ON -

They march on for some time up a hillside, murmuring amongst themselves.

NEW ANGLE ON -

The path finally opens to a majestic clearing. A large pond reflects moonlight and the hillside hovering above it.

VAN BUREN stops, and turns to his guests. He catches his breath. He is **visibly intoxicated.**

                    VAN BUREN (CONT'D)
          As you all know, these last years
          have been especially hard on Harry,
          Maggie, and myself.

ANGLE ON -

HARRY and MAGGIE give each other a squeeze, a little embarrassed.

              MAGGIE LEE
    Daddy, it's very cold out here.
    Shouldn't we go back inside?

BACK TO -

VAN BUREN stumbles but regains composure.

              VAN BUREN
    Quiet for a moment, Maggie... I
    brought you all here this evening,
    not to glance over my shoulder
    towards the past, but to invite you
    to look forward with me towards the
    future!

He points...

              VAN BUREN (CONT'D)
    On the other side of that hill is
    Doylestown. It is on this site near
    our own family plot that we plan to
    build a center for the community in
    honor of Margaret Lee Van Buren!

HARRY LEE looks distressed at the announcement.

              MICHELLE HOFFMAN
    Oh Harrison! How lovely!

The aristocrats clap a little. VAN BUREN continues...

              VAN BUREN
    This shall be a sacred enough space
    that her soul might inhabit it! A
    place for gathering, learning, and
    reflection-

He places his hand on LÁSZLÓ's shoulder.

              VAN BUREN (CONT'D)
    -and Mr. Toth, I want you to build
    this for her, something boundless,
    something new.

LÁSZLÓ blinks.

              VAN BUREN (CONT'D)
    It's a shock to you I see! I'm
    delighted! I thought you might see
    it coming!

              LÁSZLÓ
    No-

VAN BUREN throws his arm around him and starts walking him back in the direction they came.

                    VAN BUREN
          It is no coincidence that *fate*
          brought us together on the eve of
          my mother's death! I am good at
          reading the signs.

                    LÁSZLÓ
          I- I am not sure of what the
          commission entails, sir.

                    VAN BUREN
          We can discuss the details at home.
          You'll be well-compensated and
          provided a place here on the
          property to stay and work. Residing
          here will allow you the time and
          space to properly conceive of it.
          Your family, should they arrive,
          are welcome here, too. What do you
          say?

                    LÁSZLÓ
          I would like to draw something and
          present it to you.

                    VAN BUREN
               (changes gears)
          You'd prefer to win the commission?
          Fine, then do that. It's cold.
          Let's return inside.

62   **INT. VAN BUREN ESTATE FOYER - NIGHT**   62

A grandfather clock ticks. The guests have gone. LÁSZLÓ waits
on a bench under a lamp near the front door. HARRY LEE and
MAGGIE LEE can be heard having a hushed argument somewhere in
the house.

                    LÁSZLÓ
               (calls through the house)
          Excuse me!

No response.

                    LÁSZLÓ (CONT'D)
          I wonder if someone can take me to
          the train station before it gets
          too late!

                    HARRY LEE (O.S.)
               (shouts back)
          Just a moment please!

A SERVANT enters the foyer with the dirtied table cloth from
lunch. LÁSZLÓ approaches her in the hallway.

                    LÁSZLÓ
          Excuse me, sorry. A driver brought
          me here. I don't recall his name-

She doesn't speak English.

                    SERVANT
          Sorry, sorry-

                    LÁSZLÓ
          I need to get back. Can someone
          possibly contact the man who
          brought me here this afternoon?

                    SERVANT
          Just a minute please...

HARRY LEE enters from behind.

                    HARRY LEE
          Mr. Toth, I'm sorry to have kept
          you waiting.

LÁSZLÓ turns to HARRY LEE.

                    HARRY LEE (CONT'D)
          Harrison's gone to bed but he
          wishes you a good night.

Beat.

                    HARRY LEE (CONT'D)
          Listen, I am terribly sorry for my
          father's theatrics. It must have
          caught you off-guard-

                    LÁSZLÓ
               (nervous)
          That's all right...

                    HARRY LEE
          He often makes decisions without
          consulting the rest of us.

                    LÁSZLÓ
          I did not take any of it- to heart-

                    HARRY LEE
          Oh, but you *should*. You should, you
          see. My father would like us to
          hire you.

It begins to set in for LÁSZLÓ that the offer might be
sincere.

                    LÁSZLÓ
               (rambles)
          -but I have no infrastructure here.

                    HARRY LEE
          That's why he's asked me to oversee
          and assist you in this endeavor.

                    LÁSZLÓ
          I have no idea of the parameters.

                    HARRY LEE
          Once I have distilled the essence
          of father's outburst I will try and
          make some economic sense of it.

MAGGIE LEE enters.

                    MAGGIE LEE
          We've quite a full house this
          evening so I took the liberty of
          making up a place for you in the
          guest house. We can have your
          things sent for in the morning.

63   **INT. GUEST HOUSE - BEDROOM - DAY**   63

SFX: Knock, knock, knock.

ANGLE ON -

The view of the estate from the guest house window.

NEW ANGLE ON -

LÁSZLÓ wakes in a new environment, fully clothed atop some freshly ironed linens. Next to him, are all of his belongings, fetched and delivered whilst he slept. He quickly sorts through his bag to find his sketchbook.

SFX: Another round of rapping at the door...

64   **INT. VAN BUREN ESTATE - BEDROOM - LATER**   64

A SERVANT mutters something in the hallway then LÁSZLÓ cracks the door to HARRISON's sleeping chambers.

                    LÁSZLÓ (O.S.)
          You rang for me, sir?

                    VAN BUREN (O.S.)
          Come in, László! I've had a vision!

LÁSZLÓ enters with sketches in-hand.

                    LÁSZLÓ
          I have some sketches, also-
          something I have been working on
          which might be applicable here, if
          you care to look-

A NEW ANGLE reveals VAN BUREN, still in bed, an absolute wreck. He wears a sleep mask over his eyes.

                    VAN BUREN
          Stop! Stop! In a moment! My eyes
          are bleary! Take a seat!

VAN BUREN sits up in bed and pushes the sleep mask up to his forehead. He then drops something into a glass of water causing it to fizz.

> VAN BUREN (CONT'D)
> Pardon my appearance, I'll call for breakfast. I have some carpenters in the forehead causing a terrible ringing in my ears so you must bear with me-

LÁSZLÓ sits in a chair next to the bed.

> LÁSZLÓ
> I can come back-

> VAN BUREN
> Shh. Shh. Before I lose it. Dreams slip away.

LÁSZLÓ laughs.

> LÁSZLÓ
> Yes, I know.

VAN BUREN speaks methodically.

> VAN BUREN
> Doylestown is beautiful but not a cultural place, you know?

> LÁSZLÓ
> Sure.

> VAN BUREN
> But it could be. If there were an auditorium, it could host a theater festival.

> LÁSZLÓ
> Sure.

> VAN BUREN
> In the off-season, of course, the local students could access it.

> LÁSZLÓ
> Yes.

> VAN BUREN
> And what do you think of a gymnasium? I practiced wrestling as a teenager and I have fond memories of my mother accompanying me to matches in the neighboring towns.

> LÁSZLÓ
> Perhaps a swimming pool?

VAN BUREN shuts this down.

                    VAN BUREN
            I can't swim.

LÁSZLÓ remains poker-faced.

                    LÁSZLÓ
            And perhaps it's too expensive-

VAN BUREN pats LÁSZLÓ's chest affectionately.

                    VAN BUREN
                (shudders)
            Don't talk to me about money.

65   **INT. HARRY LEE'S PHILADELPHIA OFFICE - DAY**   65

MICHAEL HOFFMAN sits next to HARRY LEE red-lining a contract.

                    HARRY LEE
            Don't talk to him about money. I've
            spoken to our friends at the Bucks
            County Mayor's office who are warm
            to accessing local and state
            funding opportunities, on behalf of
            our project, if we are willing to
            designate a "specific and
            meaningful" component of the center
            for Christian congregation.

                    LÁSZLÓ
            It's a community center for all
            people. What do they want? A prayer
            room?

                    HARRY LEE
            I am under the impression they are
            expecting something more specific
            and meaningful than that for their
            earmark. This, and pending their
            approval of the overall proposal,
            of course.

LÁSZLÓ laughs a bit then realizes HARRY LEE is serious about
this casual new addition.

                    LÁSZLÓ
            An auditorium, a gymnasium, a
            library-

                    HARRY LEE
                (corrects)
            Father described it as more of *a
            reading room* for the public...

LÁSZLÓ doubles down.

                    LÁSZLÓ
            -a *library*, and a chapel? It's four
            builds, not one.

>   HARRY LEE
>   It's ambitious. Thought you'd like
>   that... I've put in a call to our
>   frequent contractor, Leslie
>   Woodrow. We first worked with
>   Leslie as one of our Ship
>   Engineering Officers but he's
>   supervised several important
>   construction projects for us since-
>   including these offices. My father
>   is allocating a sum of 850,000
>   dollars for this project which to
>   me seems very reasonable, if not
>   exorbitant. If Leslie agrees to
>   come on-board, I'll have him start
>   a budget for us right away.
>
>   MICHAEL HOFFMAN
>   This allocation of 850,000 is
>   inclusive of fees for yourself and
>   Leslie... Also, we've gone ahead
>   and made arrangements to start
>   securing you a license here in
>   Pennsylvania-

CUE: Mournful solo piano reprises over the following sequence.

66 **EXT. COUNTRY ROADS - AFTERNOON**   66

LONG LENS ON -

LÁSZLÓ rides a bicycle into town.

>   LÁSZLÓ (V.O.)
>   (in HUNGARIAN)
>   *Erzsébet,*
>   *I have become acquainted with an*
>   *influential American attorney who*
>   *says he can help you and Zsófia*
>   *with your situation.*

67 **INT. GUEST HOUSE - NIGHT**   67

CLOSE ON -

LÁSZLÓ writes a letter to his wife.

>   LÁSZLÓ (V.O.)
>   *Is there somewhere we might find a*
>   *photograph of you and Zsófia*
>   *pictured together?*

68 **EXT. DOYLESTOWN - AFTERNOON**   68

LÁSZLÓ view as he would observe the community from his bicycle.

- SCHOOL CHILDREN exit a YELLOW BUS in ULTRA SLOW-MOTION.

- A small family gather for a wedding photo outside of a local church; St. Anthony's.

- Some teens play American football in a local park in ULTRA SLOW-MOTION.

>   LÁSZLÓ (V.O.)
> *Anything linking her to you? I have reached out to colleagues who sometimes attended parties at the house. I am waiting on return.*

69   **EXT. VISTA - DUSK**   69

The sunrise... LÁSZLÓ peacefully sketches the hillside as he snacks on a healthful breakfast.

70   **EXT. VISTA - MORNING**   70

LÁSZLÓ walks the landscape's perimeter counting each click as he pushes along a Surveyor's Wheel. GORDON takes notes beside him.

>   LÁSZLÓ (V.O.)
> *Whomever comes to mind, write to them and explain its urgency. Anything tying she to you, and you to me, can be of great assistance to Mr. Hoffman. I have enclosed a list of items and information requested by his office. Please fill out what you can of these documents and return these originals to me at once.*

>   LÁSZLÓ
> 194, 195, 196, 197, 198....

>   LÁSZLÓ (V.O.)
> *Here: some good fortune may have fallen upon me. In an unexpected turn of events I have been offered an intriguing opportunity; a second chance.*

>   LÁSZLÓ
> 204, 205, 206, 207...

>   LÁSZLÓ (V.O.)
> *I can feel you nearer to me now than ever before.*

>   LÁSZLÓ
> 213, 214, 215.

LÁSZLÓ looks out over Doylestown.

>   LÁSZLÓ (V.O.)
> *Your love, László*

He begins a new calculation and begins to step off in a new direction.

> LÁSZLÓ
> 1,2,3,4,5,6,7,...

71 **INT. VAN BUREN GUEST HOUSE / DRAWING ROOM - DAY** 71

SFX: A bell chimes three times.

CLOSE ON -

"Margaret Lee Van Buren Center for Activity and Creation" is scribbled crudely at the top of the coal sketch. The semi-abstract drawing gives little indication of what the recreation center will actually look like when fully-realized. The illustration is more akin to a Jerry Hopper lithograph than a traditional architectural drawing.

LÁSZLÓ removes the sheet of paper to reveal another modular section of the structure, then a third, and fourth.

72 **INT. VAN BUREN GUEST HOUSE / DRAWING ROOM - NIGHT** 72

The living room has been transformed into a makeshift office space. By the window stands a drawing table adjusted to LÁSZLÓ's height. Paper, wooden blocks, and other materials are strewn about the room. The shades are removed from the standing lamps for better luminance.

LÁSZLÓ stands hunched over the dining room table constructing a detailed architectural model.

A SERIES OF ANGLES -

- The model: A trapezoidal structure, the centerpiece, sits atop the small hill overlooking the lake and a miniature of Doylestown on the other side.

- A cluster of buildings; sloping and irregular triangles surround the trapezoid; together they form a perfect rectangle.

- The sharp points of the model rooftops protrude out and up towards the sky.

- LÁSZLÓ carefully finishes by placing a small bell tower made of bent copper parallel to the model's main structure.

73 **EXT. VAN BUREN ESTATE FOYER - DAY** 73

LÁSZLÓ and two servants awkwardly navigate the large-scale model across the estate's horizon line.

74 INT. VAN BUREN'S STUDY - LATER

LÁSZLÓ stands at the center of VAN BUREN's study demonstrating his finished model which takes up much of the room. HARRY LEE, MAGGIE LEE and **LESLIE WOODROW** (heavy-set and above-average in height) all observe, fascinated.

VAN BUREN sits behind them all getting a haircut leafing through pages and pages of LÁSZLÓ's drawings.

> LÁSZLÓ
> The total area is 648 Square Meters, including a sizable condensate system for harvesting rainwater for the boilers below grade.

LÁSZLÓ points, gathers himself.

> LÁSZLÓ (CONT'D)
> Narrow openings at the top, as you see here and here, are skylights that can also be viewed as demarcations of units of space on either side of the entrance hall. Each unit is convertible and multi-functional with removable panels that hinge open and close. When these rooms are combined they support a total occupancy of 500 persons on each side. Bespoke systems for seating and storage allow for conference, gymnasium, auditorium. These rooms of more standard size are pre-cast concrete. The chapel at the heart of the building, however, is a perfect sphere, like a grain silo, so we'd cast on-site.

LÁSZLÓ stammers nervously.

> LÁSZLÓ (CONT'D)
> The main tower from the ground is 20 meters tall-

VAN BUREN swats his BARBER's hand away, annoyed.

> VAN BUREN
> I can't see!

HARRY clears his father's vantage point.

VAN BUREN (CONT'D)
               Harry, what do you think about the
               gymnasium off to the side like
               that? I had imagined it
               differently.

                         HARRY LEE
               It all looks like an army barracks.

Everyone waits for VAN BUREN's reaction with bated breath.

                         VAN BUREN
               Perhaps that's because you never
               enlisted, Harry. I think it's *all* a
               great surprise. Carry on, László.

LÁSZLÓ appears a bit insecure. He moves now to a different
model that demonstrates the chapel's interior.

                         LÁSZLÓ
               The Chapel's interior is more
               generous in its expression; the
               vernacular concrete contrasted by
               an altarpiece of marble from the
               mountains of Carrara will serve as
               the institute's centerpiece.

LÁSZLÓ gestures to the next model.

                         LÁSZLÓ (CONT'D)
               And see, let me demonstrate...
               Morning, midday, dusk.

ULTRA CLOSE ON -

LÁSZLÓ turns on a small flashlight and holds it at a high
angle close to the model through three entry points of light,
MAGGIE LEE, HARRY LEE and VAN BUREN lean down to look inside.
The light forms a pattern on the floor.

                         LÁSZLÓ (CONT'D)
               As the sun moves, east to west...
               Located at the base of the towers,
               wooden beams unite to form a symbol
               of the cross upon the altarpiece.

                         MAGGIE LEE
               Oh, how wonderful! The town is sure
               to be over the moon when they see
               you've kept faith and values at the
               forefront of your design.

60.

VAN BUREN
Extraordinary. Your grandmother loved marble. Maggie will you call for some coffee?

MAGGIE LEE
I think it's beautiful, Mr. Toth.

She exits. VAN BUREN looks at HARRY LEE.

LESLIE points at the towers on the right and left.

LESLIE WOODROW
(scoffs)
What's the height of those things? Six or seven meters also? And did I understand you correctly? 108 meters of surface area for the facade?! That's eleven square feet, If we can afford these materials *at all*, Mr. Van Buren, Sylacauga Marble ships out of Talladega County and that *might* be possible if I manage to swing some favors but I can't make any promises.

LÁSZLÓ
Afford these materials? The concrete is sturdy and cheap.

LESLIE speaks frankly.

LESLIE WOODROW
The concrete- it's not very attractive. Perhaps you'd like to split the difference on materials?

LÁSZLÓ
Fortunately, the building's aesthetic is not yours to resolve, Mr. Woodrow. And Sylacauga marble is *white* like a sheet of paper; it's nothing. What I have here is blue and grey with softer veining.

VAN BUREN
I prefer the Italian, I think. It's more suitable, no?

LESLIE WOODROW
I have to do some research but-

                    LÁSZLÓ
          I know someone talented, an Italian
          mason whom I have commissioned
          before.

LESLIE is visibly frustrated.

                    VAN BUREN
          There's one detail before I forget;
          the name. I'd like to place it
          somewhere more visible. What do you
          think?

LÁSZLÓ nods, lights a cigarette. MAGGIE LEE enters again
followed by two maids with trays of coffee.

                    MAGGIE LEE
              (to the maids)
          On the table over there.

MAGGIE LEE hands her father a cup and turns to LÁSZLÓ.

                    MAGGIE LEE (CONT'D)
          Sugar?

                    LÁSZLÓ
          Black.

LESLIE's eyes widen.

                    LESLIE WOODROW
          Sir, is this really what you
          imagined? Am I missing something?
          When Harry called, he described
          this to me as a personal project.
          If this is what we ultimately
          settle on, something of this scale,
          the timeline would need to be
          considerably adjusted.

                    VAN BUREN
          I'd rather be alive at 18% than
          dead at the prime rate, Leslie.

VAN BUREN winks at LESLIE.

                    LÁSZLÓ
          We will not exceed our allocation.

                    VAN BUREN
          Harry, where are we in our
          discussions with the Mayor's
          office?

                    HARRY LEE
          They are waiting on us.

                    VAN BUREN
          Push things along and see where we
          land with them.

75   **INT. GUEST HOUSE - MORNING**   75

     SFX: BANG, BANG, BANG at the door.

     LÁSZLÓ and GORDON lie in the same bed, strung out. A needle
     is still stuck in LÁSZLÓ's arm. He unties his arm and rips
     out the needle causing his arm to bleed all over the bed.

                    LÁSZLÓ
          Shit.

     SFX: BANG, BANG, BANG, again.

     LÁSZLÓ shoots up in a panic. He looks over at GORDON.

                    LÁSZLÓ (CONT'D)
          Get up.

     LÁSZLÓ pulls off a pillow case and wraps it around his elbow.

                    LÁSZLÓ (CONT'D)
               (shouts)
          Coming!

76   **EXT. GUEST HOUSE DOOR - MOMENTS LATER**   76

     LESLIE stands there impatient. After a beat, LÁSZLÓ opens the
     door.

                    LÁSZLÓ
          Morning Leslie.

                    LESLIE WOODROW
          Don't tell me you're just now
          getting up?

                    LÁSZLÓ
          Two minutes, and I am ready.

                    LESLIE WOODROW
          I'll give you three if you use it
          to rinse off.

                    LÁSZLÓ
          Three.

                    LESLIE WOODROW
          Let me inside so I can get the
          model on the truck.

77   **INT. MAYOR KINNEY'S OFFICE   - AFTERNOON**   77

LÁSZLÓ, LESLIE, and GORDON clumsily carry in the oversized model before MAYOR KINNEY, HARRY LEE and a group of other LOCAL OFFICIALS.

>   HARRY LEE
> The Mayor hasn't got all day, Leslie.

>   MAYOR KINNEY
> We're fine, Harry! Will your father be joining us, as well?

Turns to MAYOR KINNEY...

>   HARRY LEE
> He's overseas on business but he sends his regards. This is a project he's very passionate about, and a priority for us. He asked if he could telephone you to talk through it all tomorrow - at your convenience, of course?

>   MAYOR KINNEY
> Well, sure, Sylvia in my office can set for just about any time tomorrow afternoon.

>   HARRY LEE
> It will have to be in the morning due to the time difference.

>   MAYOR KINNEY
>   (sycophantic)
> Morning then is fine- just fine.

HARRY LEE and LESLIE are doing most of the talking, trying to cover for LÁSZLÓ and GORDON's bad state.

>   HARRY LEE
> They only need two minutes to set this all up.

>   LESLIE WOODROW
> We'll get this set down and start right away for ya.

The three men set the model on the table and it sadly bends down over the sides.

>   LESLIE WOODROW (CONT'D)
> You got a stool or something they can use to extend?

>   MAYOR KINNEY
> No.

>   LESLIE WOODROW
> All right, then we'll go ahead and get started.

A small figurine falls from the base of the model. LÁSZLÓ bends to the ground, sweating and catching his breath.

> LÁSZLÓ
> Apologies...

He puts the figurine back in place, uncharacteristically loose-limbed.

> MAYOR KINNEY
> (re: model)
> This is- different.

> HARRY LEE
> Very modern, yes.

> MAYOR KINNEY
> All right, well, walk us through what you have in mind.

LÁSZLÓ exhales, pulls himself together.

78 **INT. TOWN HALL - EVENING** 78

LÁSZLÓ, in formal dress, makes a speech in front of a scattered audience. Forty or so townspeople are in attendance.

> LÁSZLÓ
> Construction phase alone will create upwards of eighty local jobs. Carpenters, painters- upwards of one hundred and fifty upon completion, at which point, the facilities will need to be permanently staffed.

A TOWNSPERSON interjects...

> TOWNSPERSON (O.S.)
> (calls out)
> When are you going to answer the questions in the box?

LÁSZLÓ pauses, thinks, chooses his words carefully so as not to offend. He spots VAN BUREN in the crowd. VAN BUREN nods, encouragingly.

> LÁSZLÓ
> Yes, I- I would like also to address some of the written concerns and comments which were submitted to us anonymously ahead of tonight's discussion; questions probing my personal background, heritage, and ideological persuasion, if you will.

LÁSZLÓ clears his throat.

LÁSZLÓ (CONT'D)
As a foreign person and newcomer to Doylestown, I have observed your community with a great interest. Your town is not dissimilar to the one where I myself was raised. Your Christian church, not so different from the temple of my youth. I see your St. Anthony's decaying facade. Your school's gymnasium too slight for the size of its student body. I see a community in need and this *is my only persuasion* of relevance... Mr. Van Buren, a generous patron and practicing Protestant, *and I-* will build a place where you will be drawn to congregate and inspired to worship. You may rest assured that we will honor the traditions of Doylestown long established before I ever set foot here.

LÁSZLÓ pours himself a glass of water, takes a deliberate sip.

LÁSZLÓ (CONT'D)
I am determined to know and draw from your history and kneel upon its shoulders. Where does the structural fabric of a building appear with greater clarity than in the buildings of one's forefathers? To know and understand its nature, I have analyzed the purposes for which we build. I have examined every function which appears and determined its character. I have made its character the basis for my conception. I see the spiritual and intellectual environment of your town; The Margaret Lee Van Buren Center for Creation and Activity, will be its manifestation; a new landmark. A landmark which proclaims not only "I am new," but, "I am part of the new whole."

A SECOND TOWNSPERSON speaks up...

TOWNSPERSON 2
Excuse me, Mr...?

LÁSZLÓ
Toth.

TOWNSPERSON 2
Mr. Toth, none of us here are familiar with this type of model. Can you take us through your plans for the Recreation Center in Layman's terms? And yes; we are all keen to see what you have in mind for the chapel, especially.

LÁSZLÓ
I've had discussions with your Father Graham which informed *for me* the floor plan...

LÁSZLÓ looks at GORDON and LESLIE.

                    LÁSZLÓ (CONT'D)
         Can you pass me the flashlight?

GORDON has it at the ready. LÁSZLÓ moves the piece of model to an overhead projector and demonstrates.

                    LÁSZLÓ (CONT'D)
         Here, we have the chapel interior.
         A space suitable for 115 persons.
         At dawn...

LÁSZLÓ shines the flashlight through the southeast facing glass which casts a long *Sign of the Cross* onto the stark marble altar piece.

                    LÁSZLÓ (CONT'D)
         At *sunset*...

LÁSZLÓ shines a light down through the slits lined with copper creating an enchanting glow. The audience is audibly impressed.

PUSH IN ON VAN BUREN who is situated in the very back of the room like a proud parent.

CUE: The score booms and swells... Tympany patterns.

79   <u>**EXT. LUMBER YARD/ STEEL MANUFACTURER/ MARBLE QUARRY - VARIOUS TIMES OF DAY**</u>

Materials for the construction of the The Margaret Lee Van Buren Center for Creation and Activity are prepared around the globe.

A SERIES OF ANGLES -

- Over dramatic vistas, the sun sets.

- Steel is fabricated.

- Wood is cut and piled.

- Concrete is mixed.

- Chunks of marble are crudely sawn off in titanic fragments.

                    ERZSÉBET (V.O.)
                    (in HUNGARIAN)
         László! It has taken some months to
         obtain the items which Mr. Hoffman
         requested since receiving your
         letter. I was at first at a loss
         but suddenly thought to contact our
         upstairs neighbor in Buda, Mrs.
         Horváth! She was able to provide me
         with several family photographs
         that clearly picture you, myself,
         and Zsófia with her mother on our
         wedding day!
                    (MORE)

                    ERZSÉBET (V.O.) (CONT'D)
          *The poor dear thought us dead all
          these years so had kept them on her
          mantle in memoriam. Zsófia could
          have only been thirteen years of
          age at the time but her face and
          expression are unmistakable. I have
          included all but one in case this
          letter does not reach you. I will
          keep it near my breast, our family
          tree against my heart. László, does
          this mean we might meet again soon?
          Yours,
          Erzsébet*

The final image in the montage is a photograph of LÁSZLÓ and ERZSÉBET's wedding day. Their entire family is present. They look beautiful and happy, frozen in time.

                                              FADE IN TITLE:

                        # INTERMISSION

                              5:00 - 0:00

A yearning, nostalgic piece for piano plays over the photograph as a timer counts down from five minutes.

                                              INSERT TITLE
                                              OVER BLACK:

                            ## PART TWO
                        THE HARD CORE OF BEAUTY
                              1953-1960

80   **EXT. 30TH STREET STATION PLATFORM - MORNING**   80

LÁSZLÓ, MICHAEL and MICHELLE HOFFMAN, and MAGGIE LEE wait with flowers and balloons at the end of the platform.

LÁSZLÓ is visibly nervous. He's dressed up and shaved clean.

                    MICHELLE HOFFMAN
              Right or left?

                    MICHAEL HOFFMAN
              On the right.

                    MICHELLE HOFFMAN
              Could they have walked past us?

                    MICHAEL HOFFMAN
          My associate in New York confirmed
          they made it on.

                    MAGGIE LEE
               (points)
          There at the end, some passengers
          are still coming off.

                    LÁSZLÓ
          I see Zsófia.

He shouts and starts to move. We track left.

                    LÁSZLÓ (CONT'D)
               (shouting)
          Zsófia!

MEDIUM ON -

TWO PASSENGERS awkwardly lift ERZSÉBET's wheelchair down and
over the train steps.

                    PASSENGER
          You got her?

The PASSENGER on the left nods.

                    ERZSÉBET
          Thank you, gentlemen. We'll send
          someone for the luggage. Thank you.

                    LÁSZLÓ (O.S.)
               (shouting from some
                distance)
          Zsófia!

CLOSE ON -

ZSÓFIA, a transcendent beauty, scans the platform and begins
pushing ERZSÉBET in a wheelchair along the platform.

WE TRACK RIGHT with ERZSÉBET in profile who begins to cry at
the sound of LÁSZLÓ's voice. She's older than the wedding
photo seen prior. Her face is agonized and gaunt but her
expression betrays some optimism.

TRACK LEFT with LÁSZLÓ as his brow furrows with concern. THE
CAMERA CONTINUES TO SWING LEFT with LÁSZLÓ until they share
the frame. He bends to his wife.

                    LÁSZLÓ (CONT'D)
               (Hungarian)
          What's happened?

ERZSÉBET smiles through her tears.

                    ERZSÉBET
               (Hungarian)
          I'm sorry I didn't tell you.

                    LÁSZLÓ
                  (Hungarian)
            What happened?

                    ERZSÉBET
                  (Hungarian)
            It might not be permanent-

                    LÁSZLÓ
                  (Hungarian)
            Someone hurt you?

She cries, shakes her head.

                    ERZSÉBET
                  (Hungarian)
            It's osteoporosis from the famine-

He embraces her madly, kisses her, weeps.

                    ERZSÉBET (CONT'D)
                  (cries)
            *I can dye my hair. I know it's
            ugly.*

                    LÁSZLÓ
            Shh.

                    ERZSÉBET
                  (Hungarian)
            Where's Attila?

He switches to English.

                    LÁSZLÓ
            I didn't want him to be
            disappointed if for any reason you
            were delayed.

He looks up at ZSÓFIA and bounces up to embrace her.

                    LÁSZLÓ (CONT'D)
                  (Hungarian)
            Zsófia, dear.

He reverts again to English.

                    LÁSZLÓ (CONT'D)
            Welcome to America.

81   **INT. VAN BUREN ESTATE - DINING ROOM - LATER**   81

LÁSZLÓ, MICHAEL and MICHELLE HOFFMAN, MAGGIE LEE, and HARRY LEE all take their seats around VAN BUREN who settles at the head of the table. ERZSÉBET and ZSÓFIA hold court. Everyone appears rightfully enchanted.

                    VAN BUREN
            How wonderful it is to finally make
            your acquaintance!
                  (MORE)

VAN BUREN (CONT'D)
I admit there was a period of time when we thought he had made you up! Isn't it fascinating to meet the significant others of great artists and thinkers?

ERZSÉBET
Thank you for taking care of my László.

VAN BUREN
As persons of unique privilege, I have always thought that it is our duty to nurture the defining talents of our epoch. I possess no such talent whatsoever! Truth be told, I am terribly emulous of individuals like him.

ERZSÉBET
That mustn't be true, Mr. Van Buren. It seems you've done quite all right for yourself.

HARRY LEE
Father is digging for compliments. Don't indulge him.

Beat.

ERZSÉBET
The property is beautiful.

MAGGIE LEE
Isn't it?

VAN BUREN
Erzsébet- pardon me, am I pronouncing that correctly?

ERZSÉBET
Oh, that's fine, just fine. Feel free to call me Elizabeth if you prefer it.

VAN BUREN
Your English is impressive.

ERZSÉBET
Thank you. I attended University in England!

VAN BUREN
Where?

ERZSÉBET
Oxford to study English. I returned home for Communications.

VAN BUREN
Did you do anything with it?

ERZSÉBET
Oh yes. I wrote for a popular national paper at home; *Magyar Nemzet*.

VAN BUREN
A journalist?

HARRY LEE
Cultural?

ERZSÉBET
Foreign affairs.

ERZSÉBET turns to LÁSZLÓ.

ERZSÉBET (CONT'D)
Haven't you told them anything about me?

ERZSÉBET sees that LÁSZLÓ doesn't appreciate the joke.

CLOSE ON -

She squeezes LÁSZLÓ's hand.

BACK TO -

VAN BUREN
Perhaps you can help your poor husband to sound less like he shines shoes for a wage.

She smiles but doesn't like the joke.

VAN BUREN (CONT'D)
(to LÁSZLÓ)
How long have you been here now? Four or five years, László?! No more excuses.

VAN BUREN flips a small coin at LÁSZLÓ which LÁSZLÓ dodges. VAN BUREN laughs.

VAN BUREN (CONT'D)
All right, I got carried away! Pass that back to me, will you?

LÁSZLÓ passes it back. VAN BUREN holds it up demonstratively.

VAN BUREN (CONT'D)
A penny saved...

HARRY LEE addresses ZSÓFIA.

HARRY LEE
Sofia, is it?

LÁSZLÓ
(corrects)
Zsófia.

                    HARRY LEE
                  (pointedly)
            Zs-ófia... Are you planning for
            school?

No response. A palpable awkwardness washes over the room.
ERZSÉBET finally interjects...

                    ERZSÉBET
            She is, yes, but we haven't
            explored her options.

                    HARRY LEE
            Does she understand English?

                    ERZSÉBET
            Oh yes. She understands very well.

ERZSÉBET chooses not to elaborate. They eat in silence.

                    VAN BUREN
                  (smiles)
            "The woman behind the man."

82   **INT. VAN BUREN ESTATE - FOYER - LATER**   82

LÁSZLÓ pushes ERZSÉBET to the front door. As they are about
to leave, VAN BUREN halts their exit.

                    VAN BUREN
            László, may I have a word?

ZSÓFIA takes over for LÁSZLÓ and pushes ERZSÉBET out the
door. The two men meet at the room's most central point.

                    LÁSZLÓ
            Yes, sir?

                    VAN BUREN
            On Leslie's recommendation, we
            shared your plans with another
            architect. *Just* to get a second
            opinion - for safety reasons, as
            well.

                    LÁSZLÓ
            Who?

                    VAN BUREN
            Someone we worked with on the
            department store downtown. I forget
            his name.

VAN BUREN passes him a file.

                    VAN BUREN (CONT'D)
            Listen, they're just little
            adjustments, here and there. Places
            they thought we could save a penny.

                              LÁSZLÓ
                    Leslie is a bastard.

                              VAN BUREN
                    He is. That's what we pay him for.

83   **INT. GUEST HOUSE - HALLWAY/ ZSÓFIA'S BEDROOM - NIGHT**   83

    LÁSZLÓ takes ZSÓFIA down a corridor and opens the door
    revealing a rather childish arrangement he's made on the bed.

                              LÁSZLÓ
                         (Hungarian)
                    *I'm sorry. I remembered you as a
                    little girl.*

    ZSÓFIA touches his face and shoulder to comfort him and steps
    inside.

    LÁSZLÓ references a small framed picture of a woman.

                              LÁSZLÓ (CONT'D)
                         (Hungarian)
                    *Look at your mother. My sister was
                    beautiful, wasn't she? Even while
                    she was ill, she was so beautiful.*

    ZSÓFIA nods.

84   **INT. GUEST HOUSE CORRIDOR - LATER**   84

    LÁSZLÓ rolls ERZSÉBET down the hall to their room. Inside, he
    can heard struggling to lift her into bed.

                              LÁSZLÓ (O.S.)
                    1, 2, 3-

    She laughs adoringly.

85   **INT. GUEST HOUSE BEDROOM - LATER**   85

    ERZSÉBET and LÁSZLÓ lie catatonic in bed. It's very dark.

                              ERZSÉBET
                         (Hungarian)
                    Are you angry?

    Silence.

                              ERZSÉBET (CONT'D)
                    László, are you angry with me?

    He replies in English, petulant.

LÁSZLÓ
If you'd like to start a *row* with me, I might as well work out my English-

She replies in English.

ERZSÉBET
Stop it. Your English is perfectly all right. It was an unimaginative joke he made about you shining shoes.

LÁSZLÓ
Tomorrow, I'll take you to see someone. A specialist.

ERZSÉBET
Don't be angry with me.

LÁSZLÓ sulks..

ERZSÉBET (CONT'D)
Do you not want to be with me anymore?

LÁSZLÓ
Stop this nonsense.

ERZSÉBET
Do you think I look older?

LÁSZLÓ
We *are* older.

ERZSÉBET
Can't you say anything kind to me?

LÁSZLÓ
I love you, you cow.

ERZSÉBET smiles and kisses him.

ERZSÉBET
(Hungarian, whispers)
You can touch me.

LÁSZLÓ
I don't want to hurt you- physically.

ERZSÉBET
You won't... I had dreams- every night, I dreamt I was with you.

She touches him under the sheets.

ERZSÉBET (CONT'D)
I know what you've done, László, and it's all right...

                    LÁSZLÓ
          What are you talking about?

                    ERZSÉBET
               (whispers)
          László, I know. I know. I know
          everything. You see, I became sick.
          Very sick. I could hardly breathe.
          I yearned to be with you and it
          made me sick. I almost died.
          Between life and death, I began
          having fantasies about you but I
          realized they were not fantasies at
          all, but *visions*! I was with you.
          All the time I was with you.

She licks her palm, jerks him off, whispers in his ear.

                    ERZSÉBET (CONT'D)
          László, I know what you've done.
          I'm not jealous because I was with
          you the all the time. I know
          everything that has happened to
          you, and I am here now and I will
          never leave you.

LÁSZLÓ breaks down. His voice cracks in heaving sobs.

                    LÁSZLÓ
          *Oh god! MY LOVE. MY LOVE! I CANNOT
          BEAR IT!*

                    ERZSÉBET
          You can. Shh... You can. We have a
          new life. A new language. We can
          start again.

86   **INT. GUEST HOUSE - CORRIDOR/ BATHROOM - MORNING**   86

LÁSZLÓ walks down the corridor and opens the door to discover
ZSÓFIA guiding ERZSÉBET's knee to her chest who lies nude in
the tub wearing a hair net. They both flush with
embarrassment at the sight of LÁSZLÓ. ERZSÉBET laughs as she
tries to cover up.

                    LÁSZLÓ
          Sorry.

He quickly steps back the way he came.

                    ERZSÉBET (O.S.)
          Maggie Lee lent me some hair
          product!

87   **INT. GUEST HOUSE - MOMENTS LATER**   87

LÁSZLÓ takes a coffee in his kitchenette reviewing VAN
BUREN's file. He furrows his brow.

                    ERZSÉBET (O.S.)
                (calls out)
            László, are you there?

He regards ZSÓFIA exercising her aunt in the bathtub through
the door ajar.

                    LÁSZLÓ
                (calls back)
            I am.

                    ERZSÉBET (O.S.)
                (calls out)
            The model is beautiful, darling! So
            beautiful.

LÁSZLÓ regards the model.

                    ERZSÉBET (CONT'D)
            We're taking a bus into the city
            this afternoon to visit Attila. The
            stop is very nearby! Would you like
            to come?

                    LÁSZLÓ
            I have something this afternoon.

88   **INT. GUEST HOUSE - BATHROOM - SAME**   88

ERZSÉBET smiles at ZSÓFIA, full of joy.

                    ERZSÉBET
            I've missed him. Just hearing him
            mill about in the other room.
            It's...

ERZSÉBET searches for the right word.

                    ERZSÉBET (CONT'D)
            Fantastic.

89   **INT. VAN BUREN ESTATE - LOUNGE - LATER**   89

VAN BUREN observes the front yard from the quietude of his
private quarters. He watches...

LONG LENS ON -

ZSÓFIA and ERZSÉBET explore the property. ZSÓFIA pushes
ERZSÉBET's wheelchair through the estate's hedge maze.
ERZSÉBET says something to make ZSÓFIA crack a smile.

90   **EXT. VAN BUREN ESTATE - DRIVEWAY - LATER**   90

WE TRACK RIGHT with ZSÓFIA and ERZSÉBET who have put on
something more formal for their outing into town. ZSÓFIA
pushes ERZSÉBET at a steady clip.

                    ERZSÉBET
          Perhaps we should see about some
          language classes this afternoon?
          You could take the bus in on your
          own...

ZSÓFIA hardly reacts.

                    ERZSÉBET (CONT'D)
          I am *positive* it is the last place
          you would like to be but it's good
          for you and I can brief the
          instructor or whomever about your
          situation. Listening to me babble
          on will only get you so far.

After some time, VAN BUREN's town car pulls up beside them.
He rolls the window down...

                    VAN BUREN
          Where are you two headed?

                    ERZSÉBET
          We're going into town.

                    VAN BUREN
          Which town is that? We've got
          several nearby, you know!

ERZSÉBET laughs pleasantly.

                    ERZSÉBET
          Philadelphia. To visit family.

                    VAN BUREN
          Ah, yes. The American cousin! The
          city then! Us, as well.

ERZSÉBET corrects herself.

                    ERZSÉBET
          Yes, the city.

                    VAN BUREN
               (to ZSÓFIA)
          Well, don't just stand there. Let
          us give you and your Auntie a lift.

VAN BUREN opens the door to the backseat and steps out to
help move ERZSÉBET inside.

91   **INT. AUTOMOBILE - MOMENTS LATER**   91

VAN BUREN sits in the passenger side front seat. The two
ladies sit in the back.

                    VAN BUREN
          I have a friend in New York, a
          newspaper man. He's always on the
          lookout for new talent. Shall I
          mention you to him?

ERZSÉBET
Well, yes, of course. That is very kind of you, Mr. Van Buren.

ERZSÉBET thinks, hesitates, then...

ERZSÉBET (CONT'D)
Would that mean I would have to work out of New York?

VAN BUREN
In the beginning, perhaps... But you haven't got the job yet so let's not get ahead of ourselves.

ERZSÉBET
No, no, of course not. I did not mean it to be presumptuous!

The road is rough and the engine, loud.

VAN BUREN
What's that?

ERZSÉBET
(shouts to be heard)
I did not mean it to be presumptuous!

VAN BUREN accepts her acknowledgement and moves on.

VAN BUREN
In any event, you could commute there with me at the start. I'm there Monday to Friday.

ERZSÉBET
Well, sure, that could be fine. I'd have to speak with László though.

VAN BUREN
When we break ground, he will have his hands full, I can assure you!

VAN BUREN's intent is enigmatic.

VAN BUREN (CONT'D)
I enjoy showing friends around Manhattan. You mustn't have seen much on your way in.

ERZSÉBET
The Penn Station Terminal was very nice.

VAN BUREN
-a pity that it's become so full of tramps hassling women and children with their arms outstretched. They line up and extend from the walls as if integral to its very foundation like-

He searches for the apt metaphor.

VAN BUREN (CONT'D)
-like a haunted wall mural!

ERZSÉBET
Ah, perhaps that is why I felt so *at home*. I'm a former bag lady myself who does also enjoy the work of the Dutch masters.

VAN BUREN
'Earthly Delights!' You pictured it just as I meant it. Clever, clever.

ERZSÉBET looks at her niece with some trepidation about the conversation then digs deeper.

ERZSÉBET
"Integral to its foundation." You sound like my husband. Although a mural's decorative; nothing to do with the foundation.

The jab doesn't seem to land. No response from VAN BUREN. They ride in silence for a moment. It's unclear whether or not he's taken offense.

ERZSÉBET (CONT'D)
Where did you get your passion for architecture?

VAN BUREN
Oh, we've done buildings before but I'd hardly call them artistic. I suppose it was because the cellar was full.

ERZSÉBET
Pardon?

VAN BUREN
I collect books, butterflies, and such. Above all though, Portuguese Madeira. I take it every night after supper.

He turns to her.

VAN BUREN (CONT'D)
I did the *maths* and if I were to uncork a bottle seven days a week for the next thirty years - the maximum of my life expectancy - I shouldn't need more than ten thousand altogether. So once the cellar was full, it was time I set about in a new *direction.* Out of the cellar and into the sky.

ERZSÉBET
If you drink a bottle of Madeira every day, I shouldn't think you'd last thirty years.

                    VAN BUREN
          I always keep good company.

ERZSÉBET senses VAN BUREN asserting himself, flirting with
her.

92   **EXT. VISTA - CONSTRUCTION SITE - TRAILERS - DAY**   92

WE TRACK FAST RIGHT with LÁSZLÓ who trembles with anger.

93   **INT. VISTA - CONSTRUCTION SITE - OFFICE TRAILER - CONTINUOUS**   93

LÁSZLÓ enters the trailer where LESLIE WOODROW is on a
telephone call. **LÁSZLÓ throws the file at LESLIE's head...**

                    LESLIE WOODROW
          I'm going to have to call you back.

LESLIE hangs up the phone.

                    LÁSZLÓ
          How dare you.

                    LESLIE WOODROW
          How dare I what?

LÁSZLÓ's accent is embellished when he is angry.

                    LÁSZLÓ
          You go behind the back- and have
          them meet with another goddamned
          designer! Who in the hell is James
          T. Simpson? You're trying to get me
          sacked!

                    LESLIE WOODROW
          I didn't tell him to meet with
          anyone. Of course, I didn't. You
          think I feel like working with you
          hating my guts for the next two
          godforsaken years?

LÁSZLÓ blinks.

                    LESLIE WOODROW (CONT'D)
          Jim Simpson is a smart guy. He
          doesn't want to interfere at all.

LÁSZLÓ taps the document with his index finger.

                    LÁSZLÓ
          I'm not making these changes.

                    LESLIE WOODROW
          I'm afraid it's not up to you. The
          casts are already finished. We put
          in that order over a month ago.
          This is the first time you're
          hearing about it?

                    LÁSZLÓ
          No one told me a damned thing.

                    LESLIE WOODROW
          Harrison said he would talk it over
          with you. I'm sorry you found out
          this way. I really am.

LÁSZLÓ sits down and starts re-drawing the plans in a fever.

He makes new connections, new corridors, new ideas, with a
few strokes of a pen then slams it down in front of LESLIE.

                    LÁSZLÓ
          There. It's mine again. He cuts
          three meters from the top, I add it
          to the bottom!

                    LESLIE WOODROW
          We can't afford all this! I'm
          already over-budget this quarter!

                    LÁSZLÓ
          Use what you need to of my fee.

LESLIE tries to reason with him.

                    LESLIE WOODROW
          What's the difference between forty
          and fifty feet, anyway?! The
          ceilings are still plenty high!

                    LÁSZLÓ
          Get it approved, Leslie.

                    LESLIE WOODROW
          We have a walk-thru next week and
          Jim is supposed to be there. Just
          hear him out. You can state your
          case to Harrison and Harry Lee. I
          won't open my mouth, I swear it.

94   **EXT. VISTA - CONSTRUCTION SITE - TRENCHES - MORNING**   94

It's raining cats and dogs. Thunder, lightning, wind.

ULTRA-WIDE ANGLE TRACKING SHOT -

SEVEN MEN; LÁSZLÓ, VAN BUREN, HARRY LEE, LESLIE WOODROW,
MAYOR KINNEY, MICHAEL HOFFMAN, and **JIM SIMPSON** stand in the
newly dug out foundation; a corridor of dirt reminiscent of
the First War trenches.

They all hold out large canvas umbrellas to shield themselves
from the torrential downpour.

                    LÁSZLÓ
          For the cantilevered floors- we
          plan to use upside-down T-shaped
          beams integrated into concrete
          slabs down here.
                    (MORE)

                    LÁSZLÓ (CONT'D)
               This will form both the ceiling of
               the space below and provide
               resistance against compression...

MAYOR KINNEY tries to make sense of the blueprints.

                    MAYOR KINNEY
               Which corridor are we in now?

LESLIE nervously tries to explain...

                    LESLIE WOODROW
               We're below ground here. It's a
               sort of- passageway between the
               main unit and the three mid-sized
               modular units to the south and
               southeast.

JIM SIMPSON reviews LÁSZLÓ's new plans...

                    JIM SIMPSON
               I don't see how any of this
               acknowledges my proposed cuts. We
               are just spinning our wheels out
               here. I took ten feet off the
               height of these damned things and
               now we are 30 feet underground?! I
               mean, what is- what are all these
               new connections between facilities?

                    LÁSZLÓ
               A better idea.

                    JIM SIMPSON
               What are they for? You put all
               these together and you've added on
               a quarter mile or so of tunnel to
               carve out on top of everything
               else!

LÁSZLÓ keeps his cool. He speaks to be heard but never shouts explaining himself to the group.

                    LÁSZLÓ
               We excavate the entire diameter of
               the tunnel system using a- full-
               face method.

                    JIM SIMPSON
               For what?! Why can't people just
               walk themselves directly across the
               courtyard?!

                    LÁSZLÓ
               Something inside for the people to
               discover.

LÁSZLÓ is starting to get as worked up as we have ever seen him.

                    LÁSZLÓ (CONT'D)
               And so it is one building and not
               four! For its <u>harmony</u>. You said it
               before, Mr. Van Buren!
                         (MORE)

> LÁSZLÓ (CONT'D)
> You expected it to be one building, and now it is!

VAN BUREN nods, uncomfortable. JIM SIMPSON scoffs.

> JIM SIMPSON
> I'll tell you- we are not going back inside until you look us in the eye and you tell us where you are willing to compromise?!

LÁSZLÓ seethes but remains calm.

> LÁSZLÓ
> Jim, tell us again what you've built?

> JIM SIMPSON
> I'll tell you about what I've built, whatever-the-hell-your-name-is! A shopping center in New Hope, a hotel in Stamford Connecticut-

LESLIE INTERJECTS...

> LESLIE WOODROW
> Now Jim, let me remind everyone that László has offered to personally off-set these costs-

> JIM SIMPSON
> You brought me in here to tell you what it is that you do not need! You don't need this guy!

JIM SIMPSON points at LÁSZLÓ, accusingly.

> JIM SIMPSON (CONT'D)
> This whole thing is just- bizarre, Leslie!

> LESLIE WOODROW
> I really think you two might see eye-to-eye if you just spent a little more time getting to know each other. Honestly.

JIM throws his papers up in the air.

> LÁSZLÓ
> Jim. Listen to me.

> JIM SIMPSON
> I'm listening.

> LÁSZLÓ
> Everything we see that is ugly- stupid, cruel, and ugly. Everything is your fault.

Taking a moment to fully digest the severity of LÁSZLÓ's sentiment, **JIM SIMPSON replies with a violent push causing LÁSZLÓ to slip and fall in the mud.**

                    VAN BUREN
          Jim, you stop that right now!

JIM SIMPSON appears embarrassed.

                    JIM SIMPSON
          I'm sorry-

                    VAN BUREN
          Think it's time for you to head
          home, Jim. Thanks for your insight.

JIM SIMPSON walks away. VAN BUREN extends a hand to LÁSZLÓ.

                    VAN BUREN (CONT'D)
          I trust you. I trust you, all
          right?

95   **EXT. VISTA - CONSTRUCTION SITE - MOMENTS LATER**   95

MAYOR KINNEY walks ahead of the group with VAN BUREN.

                    MAYOR KINNEY
          Are you sure about this guy? I know
          Jim lost his temper but he had a
          few points back there, didn't he?
          My office is fielding complaints
          about the plans for this place on a
          daily basis, more or less! Jim's a
          Protestant! Gives folks peace of
          mind. People are worried it's going
          to ruin the hillside, Harrison.

                    VAN BUREN
          We'll do something. A little event
          for the community. Get them on-
          side.

VAN BUREN's expression doesn't betray his intent.

                    VAN BUREN (CONT'D)
          And Jim will stay on.

MAYOR KINNEY furrows his brow.

                    MAYOR KINNEY
          Does Jim know that? I think he
          thinks he's fired.

                    VAN BUREN
          I'll have Leslie telephone him
          tomorrow, and Jim can advise from
          afar.

VAN BUREN gestures to LÁSZLÓ behind them.

                    VAN BUREN (CONT'D)
          It's better for morale this way,
          you see?

96   **EXT. VISTA - AFTERNOON**   96

The sun is shining. A small crowd has gathered for a ribbon cutting ceremony. VAN BUREN, HARRY LEE, and LÁSZLÓ pose for a photograph with MAYOR KINNEY. Following a round of pictures, VAN BUREN calls out...

                    VAN BUREN
          Girls! Girls! Come in for a
          picture!

ERZSÉBET, ZSÓFIA, MAGGIE LEE enter from the side and gather around the core group. ERZSÉBET tugs at LÁSZLÓ's blazer and he obliges by kneeling down to her chair. She whispers in his ear...

                    ERZSÉBET
               (Hungarian, whispers)
          *I'm proud of you. Make love to me
          tonight.*

VAN BUREN holds up a shovel demonstratively.

                    VAN BUREN
          All right everyone! On three...

                    EVERYONE
          O-ne! T-wo!

Everyone but ZSÓFIA smiles.

                    VAN BUREN
          And...

He pulls the shovel back.

                    EVERYONE
          Three!

The shovel breaks the earth.

97   **EXT. VISTA - WATERING HOLE - DUSK**   97

CLOSE HANDHELD ON -

The sun is setting. Several party guests are swimming. It's exactly like a Renoir. Sun-drenched ZSÓFIA bathes sensually in the pond, her skin tightens with goosebumps. HARRY LEE swims up to greet her.

                    HARRY LEE
               (cheerful)
          *Rub-a-dub, three maids in a tub.
          And who do you think were there?
          The butcher, the baker, the
          candlestick-maker-*

He takes some water in his mouth and spits it out.

                    HARRY LEE (CONT'D)
          Invigorating, isn't it?

NEW ANGLE ON -

By the shore, ERZSÉBET lies on a towel near LÁSZLÓ, VAN BUREN, and MAGGIE LEE. All of them laugh madly; a joyous scene.

          ERZSÉBET
          (hysterical)
    Did you ever manage to find the
    place?

          MAGGIE LEE
    After driving around for hours in
    the dark looking for this damned
    camouflaged mailbox-

MAGGIE LEE laughs in anticipation of the punchline as she recounts the story.

      MAGGIE LEE (CONT'D)   VAN BUREN
-we walked in the door, and   (interjects)
the table had just been   It was well after ten o'clock-
cleared for dessert!

          ERZSÉBET
    -and then what?!

          MAGGIE LEE
    I noticed something a little *funny*
    about the other dinner guests.

          ERZSÉBET
    How so?!

          MAGGIE LEE
    They just all looked a bit pale in
    the face, I reckon...

Even LÁSZLÓ can't help but grin now.

          ERZSÉBET
    OH NO!

          VAN BUREN
    Maggie, you're exaggerating.

          MAGGIE LEE
    I AM NOT, I swear it! They looked
    exactly like that popular painting,
    you know the one-?

MAGGIE LEE imitates Edvard Munch's 'The Scream' causing another fit of laughter.

          ERZSÉBET
    Stop it! I can't breathe.

MAGGIE LEE
Daddy kept apologizing to our hostess-

VAN BUREN
For context, her husband is among *Van Buren Steel's* most important private clients.

MAGGIE LEE
Daddy tried to explain everything that had made us late as she prepared for us *what appeared* to be a delightful looking little trifle!

ERZSÉBET
Was it awful?

MAGGIE LEE
I kid you not; cow tallow and fruit pie!

ERZSÉBET
(laughs)
NO!

MAGGIE LEE
-and poor daddy has such a sweet tooth! I didn't know how to warn him in front of everyone before he took a bite this big!

MAGGIE demonstrates the enormous slice with her index fingers.

ERZSÉBET
(to VAN BUREN)
NO!

VAN BUREN
Indeed.

MAGGIE LEE
He began gagging like a house cat!

She imitates a house cat gagging on a fur ball.

MAGGIE LEE (CONT'D)
And all he could say to explain was...

MAGGIE LEE holds herself together for the finale.

MAGGIE LEE (CONT'D)
'Dear... I am allergic.' to which our concerned hostess replied, *' allergic to what?!'*, and he says...

VAN BUREN buries his face in hands.

MAGGIE LEE (CONT'D)
'TO THAT. I am very allergic to whatever THAT is.'

Everyone howls.

98   **EXT. VISTA - LATER**   98

LONG LENS ON -

ZSÓFIA and HARRY LEE come up from the water and stand beside VAN BUREN, MAGGIE LEE, and ÉRZSÉBET who is now situated back in her wheelchair.

NEW ANGLE ON -

LÁSZLÓ regards them but stands talking with GORDON and GORDON's son, **WILLIAM** (significantly older than when we last saw him). **The three of them observe a small construction crew that carry futons above their heads which implies they'll be sleeping on-site.**

WILLIAM points.

                    WILLIAM
          Is that your crew?

                    GORDON
          They'll sleep here.

                    WILLIAM
          It's a lot of them. (Beat) What's
          that thing over there?

                    GORDON
          On the left?

WILLIAM nods.

                    GORDON (CONT'D)
          That's a motor grader. We used to
          do it with horses. Makes a flat
          surface to pour on.

                    LÁSZLÓ
          We can take you down there in the
          morning if you are curious.

GORDON squeezes his son.

                    GORDON
          What do you say we get you in one
          of them machines?

                    HARRY LEE (O.S.)
          Big day, Mr. Toth!

HARRY LEE approaches the scene.

                    LÁSZLÓ
          Yes.

HARRY LEE, drunk but not sloppy, puts an arm around LÁSZLÓ and WE TRACK with them as they walk off.

HARRY LEE
Leslie mentioned during our meeting last week with Jim that you're putting your fee back into the project. That seems a bit irresponsible given your situation, doesn't it? Will it even last you to the end of your commitment?

LÁSZLÓ is silent, then...

LÁSZLÓ
I will figure something out.

HARRY LEE
Have you discussed it with your wife?

LÁSZLÓ
She will be supportive.

HARRY LEE
Suit yourself but I wouldn't do it, and I know Leslie *certainly* wouldn't do it, so I didn't want you to think you'd be setting any sort of precedent.

LÁSZLÓ
I expect nothing from either of you.

BEAT.

LÁSZLÓ (CONT'D)
How does that work exactly? The company paying themselves to finance?

HARRY LEE
Do you not think I deserve to be paid for the time and energy I devote to this project?

The question hangs in the air as they come to a stop.

HARRY LEE (CONT'D)
Might I make a suggestion?

LÁSZLÓ
You may.

HARRY LEE
Your niece has made several of our guests very uncomfortable. Perhaps you should have a talk with her.

LÁSZLÓ
About what?

                    HARRY LEE
          Don't get me wrong. She's very
          lovely to look at and as much as we
          all dream of having a bird that
          keeps her trap shut, it comes off
          like a rude affectation. I've tried
          to connect, make conversation. It
          goes nowhere.

LÁSZLÓ doesn't respond.

                    HARRY LEE (CONT'D)
          Oh, I see. It must run in the
          family.

No response.

                    HARRY LEE (CONT'D)
          I would like us to be friends...

                    LÁSZLÓ
          This is not- friendly, Harry.

HARRY LEE lets go, exasperated.

                    HARRY LEE
          I didn't say I'd like to slip my
          prick into her. Forget it! I've had
          too much to drink. I need a nap.

HARRY LEE begins to walk off and turns around to share a
final sentiment.

                    HARRY LEE (CONT'D)
                (venomous)
          We tolerate you.

99   **EXT. VISTA - MOMENTS LATER**   99

LÁSZLÓ approaches ERZSÉBET, ZSÓFIA, and VAN BUREN.

                    LÁSZLÓ
          It's time for us to go.

                    VAN BUREN
          You don't want to join us for
          dinner at the house?

                    LÁSZLÓ
          We start early tomorrow. Thanks for
          the event.

                    VAN BUREN
                (to ERZSÉBET)
          Does he ever take a rest?

                    ERZSÉBET
          Never. Good night, Mr. Van Buren.

LÁSZLÓ turns ERZSÉBET in her chair and WE TRACK with them
back towards the main property. ZSÓFIA follows...

                    ERZSÉBET (CONT'D)
          What's the rush?

                    LÁSZLÓ
          We can talk at the house.

                    ERZSÉBET
          Can you slow down?

                    LÁSZLÓ
               (matter-of-fact)
          I am forfeiting the remainder of my
          fee due to some expenses
          unforeseen.

                    ERZSÉBET
          So, that's what the son kept
          alluding to.

                    LÁSZLÓ
          Yes. He's a snake.

LÁSZLÓ regards ZSÓFIA just next to him.

                    LÁSZLÓ (CONT'D)
               (*Hungarian*)
          Don't go near him Zsófia.

ZSÓFIA nods, appreciative of her uncle's sentiment.

                    ERZSÉBET
          All right, so what will that mean
          for us?

                    LÁSZLÓ
          I will figure something out.

                    ERZSÉBET
          We will figure something out. I
          suppose we can make due on my
          salary.

                    LÁSZLÓ
          -your salary?

ERZSÉBET's tone is playful though her voice does quiver with
some concern.

                    ERZSÉBET
          Mr. Van Buren's helped me with a
          job interview in New York City. I'm
          sure once they meet me, they won't
          be able to resist me.

100   **INT. GUEST HOUSE - NIGHT**   100

LÁSZLÓ, ERZSÉBET, ZSÓFIA, GORDON, and WILLIAM sit for a
peasant's supper that ERZSÉBET's prepared for them.

GORDON
Thank you for the supper, Mrs. Toth.

ERZSÉBET
I thought we might have our own little party to celebrate all of your hard work. You've come so far, the both of you.

GORDON
Oh, it's not mine really.

ERZSÉBET
(pointedly)
That's not what László tells me. He says he couldn't have done it without you.

LÁSZLÓ looks a little embarrassed at the affection he's expressed in private for his colleague and friend.

ERZSÉBET (CONT'D)
Do you have a misses at home, Gordon?

GORDON
(mournful)
William's mother, Augusta, passed away in '43- she got sick and died of a damned tooth infection of all things.

ERZSÉBET directs her attention to WILLIAM.

ERZSÉBET
I am very sorry to hear that, and I am terribly sorry for your loss.

GORDON
He's all right. He was too young then to remember much, and I was gone training two years in Arizona before they shipped us all off to Naples, Italy; 92nd Infantry Division. They wouldn't let me back home all that time, not once. Augusta's sister looked after him until I got back. Kept me alive though, knowing he was waiting for me.

GORDON puts a hand on his teenage son's back.

GORDON (CONT'D)
Kept me good and alive, thank goodness.

ERZSÉBET blurts out.

ERZSÉBET
Zsofia's mother passed.

ZSÓFIA, previously emotive, turns to stone.

ERZSÉBET (CONT'D)
Losing a mother- it's an unfathomable loss, you see. To lose one's birth mother is to lose the very foundation on which we stand.

ERZSÉBET turns to WILLIAM...

ERZSÉBET (CONT'D)
The mind may not know its loss but the heart does.

WILLIAM finally speaks for himself.

WILLIAM
I remember her.

GORDON
That's because I've told you so much about her. You were too small.

WILLIAM is defiant.

WILLIAM
No, I remember Augusta. I just wanted to make it easier on you.

101 **INT. GUEST HOUSE - LIVING ROOM - LATER** 101

ERZSÉBET smokes leafing through her husband's drawings. After some time, LÁSZLÓ enters from behind her...

LÁSZLÓ
What are you doing?

She doesn't turn around to regard him. She keeps observing what's in front of her.

ERZSÉBET
Oh, I'm just looking at you.

LÁSZLÓ smiles, kisses the back of her neck.

LÁSZLÓ
What do you think?

ERZSÉBET
It's unusual. Even for you.

LÁSZLÓ
You think so?

ERZSÉBET
Many rooms are quite small. The ceilings are high...

LÁSZLÓ
Yes. Inside, you must look upwards.

                    ERZSÉBET
          So, which part of it are we paying
          for?

                    LÁSZLÓ
          The height of the ceilings. The
          glass above.

102   **EXT. VISTA - DAY**   102

      VARIOUS ANGLES OF MEN AT WORK. The vista has transformed into
      an active construction site on a grand scale. LÁSZLÓ and
      GORDON supervise as their crew lays the rest of the concrete
      foundation.

      INT. THE CONGREGATION MIKVEH ISRAEL - MIKVEH

      LÁSZLÓ, ERZSÉBET, ZSÓFIA, and MICHAEL & MICHELLE HOFFMAN file
      into a corridor towards the basement that's been set up for a
      makeshift service at Yom Kippur. ERZSÉBET laughs a bit at the
      banal functionality of their surroundings.

                    ERZSÉBET
          The service is in here?

      MICHELLE HOFFMAN nods.

                    MICHELLE HOFFMAN
                      (clarifies)
          For the overflow.

                    ERZSÉBET
          Because of the holiday?

                    MICHELLE HOFFMAN
          The community is growing.

      INT. THE CONGREGATION MIKVEH ISRAEL - LATER

      LÁSZLÓ and MICHAEL HOFFMAN wear Talith reciting the Viddui,
      rhythmically pounding their chests in accordance with the
      prayer.

                    LÁSZLÓ AND MICHAEL
                      (chanting in *Hebrew*)
          We have stolen, slandered, sinned…
          We were wicked, malicious, have
          taken, and lied
          We've been evil and given harmful
          advice…

      LÁSZLÓ hits his chest with considerable force.

105   **EXT. TRAIN DEPOT - MORNING**   105

      Crew men load monolithic slabs of pre-cast concrete onto a
      flat bed train car.

                              MEN
                     Careful, careful!

106   **EXT. MEADOW - RAILROAD - EVENING**   106

        CUE: The score imitates the Hebrew Cantillation. It swells,
        magnificent.

                            LÁSZLÓ (O.S.)
                         (chanting in Hebrew)
                      We have deceived, mocked-

        ULTRA-WIDE ON -

        In the distance, a long train, made small by the landscape.
        Peace and beauty.

                            LÁSZLÓ (CONT'D)
                      Rebelled, against god, against
                      others,
                      We are spiteful.

        ANGLE ON -

        The tracks rush at us on a wide-angle lens.

                            LÁSZLÓ (CONT'D)
                      We have turned away,
                      Deliberately.

        BACK TO ULTRA-WIDE -

        The train derails and explosions appear in the smoke from the
        steam engine... The event is catastrophic but we are so far
        away that it hardly makes a sound.

107   **INT. GUEST HOUSE BEDROOM - NIGHT**   107

        ERZSÉBET wakes up in bed wailing. LÁSZLÓ is alert, terrified.

                            LÁSZLÓ
                     What's happening?!

                            ERZSÉBET
                     It's too much!

                            LÁSZLÓ
                     What's too much?!

        She lets out another primal scream.

                            ERZSÉBET
                     The pain is too much. I need
                     Zsófia! She has my medication.

        LÁSZLÓ stumbles out of bed and exits. ERZSÉBET writhes in the
        sheets.

108   INT. VISTA - CONSTRUCTION SITE - OFFICE TRAILER - DAY   108

LÁSZLÓ, HARRY LEE, VAN BUREN, and two ENGINEERS are huddled into the back of a makeshift office space on the lot. LESLIE WOODROW holds a telephone to his ear...

> LESLIE WOODROW
> I have everyone here with me now, yes.

Beat.

> LESLIE WOODROW (CONT'D)
> I see. Well, please let us know if there is anything at all we can do. We are terribly sorry for the news.

Beat.

> LESLIE WOODROW (CONT'D)
> On tenterhooks at this end so give me a ring here when you have something.

LESLIE hangs up the phone.

> LESLIE WOODROW (CONT'D)
> A big section came undone, he couldn't tell me which one for certain, and it took seven freight cars along with it.

VAN BUREN slams his hands on the desk.

> VAN BUREN
> (shouts)
> How the hell did you find these people, Leslie?!

> HARRY LEE
> Transpo company is our own, Dad-

> VAN BUREN
> WHAT?!

> HARRY LEE
> We sent our own guys to Charleston.

> LESLIE WOODROW
> The rail cars were ours too... It was cheaper given all the back and forth. It's well over a hundred shipments, Harrison.

> VAN BUREN
> You don't utter another goddamned word to the rail company until Michael can advise.

> LESLIE WOODROW
> I'm hoping to have more answers for you soon, sir.

LÁSZLÓ
How far is it? Can we see what can be salvaged?

LESLIE WOODROW
The accident put two brakemen in the hospital. It's a real mess out there.

VAN BUREN
Send their families flowers for Christ's sake-

Beat.

VAN BUREN (CONT'D)
Wait. Don't. Looks guilty.

HARRY LEE
I'll call Michael.

HARRY LEE exits.

LESLIE WOODROW
What would you like me to do in the meantime?

VAN BUREN
With what?

LESLIE WOODROW
Our crew.

VAN BUREN
Let them go.

LÁSZLÓ looks sick.

LÁSZLÓ
Sir, you can't-

VAN BUREN
I CAN! YES! YES, I CAN!

VAN BUREN paces furiously.

VAN BUREN (CONT'D)
People are going to write about this! I'm staring down the barrel of the next two years of my goddamned life, Mr. Toth! What if one of them dies? What if both of them die? Who's going to pay for it? Are you going to pay for it?!

LESLIE WOODROW
László, in the interest of transparency, before I came to retrieve you, I had already advised Mr. Van Buren to cut his losses-

                    VAN BUREN
          Shut up, Leslie.

     LESLIE swallows, humiliated. VAN BUREN exhales.

                    LÁSZLÓ
          Sir, please.

                    VAN BUREN
          Don't beg. It's unbecoming. You're
          welcome to stay here until you've
          found your footing elsewhere. I
          have a mess to clean up.

109   **EXT. VISTA - CONSTRUCTION SITE - MOMENTS LATER**   109

     We track left fast with LÁSZLÓ and GORDON across the
     landscape.

                    LÁSZLÓ
          I'm sorry, Gordon.

                    GORDON
          Don't apologize to me.

                    LÁSZLÓ
          I can give you some money while you
          look for something.

                    GORDON
          I'll be fine.

                    LÁSZLÓ
               (affirmative)
          You have a kid. I'll give you
          something and you'll take it.

     LÁSZLÓ stops in his tracks and looks at GORDON.

                    LÁSZLÓ (CONT'D)
          You got any *hop* on you?

     GORDON looks grave.

                    GORDON
          None at all. I'm off it.

                    LÁSZLÓ
          Good, good. That's good to hear.

110   **INT. GUEST HOUSE - LATER**   110

     LÁSZLÓ smashes the model in a terrible fury. ERZSÉBET
     observes her husband's tantrum, unmoved.

                    ERZSÉBET
          You're making me a mess to clean
          up.

He continues on...

> ERZSÉBET (CONT'D)
> (shouts)
> STOP IT! You're acting like a child.

> LÁSZLÓ
> It's over.

> ERZSÉBET
> You have to march over there *right now* and get him excited again. Keep him engaged. You know how these rich fellows are. For him, it's like refurbishing *a kitchen*.

> LÁSZLÓ
> Two people are in the hospital.

> ERZSÉBET
> That's not your fault–

> LÁSZLÓ
> Darling, it's over.

Silence.

FADE TO BLACK.

111 **EXT. NEW YORK CITY'S MIDTOWN EAST (MURRAY HILL) - DAY** 111

VIEW FROM THE EAST RIVER TOWARDS THE UNITED NATIONS AND THE SURROUNDING NEW YORK CITY SKYLINE.

CROSS DISSOLVE:

INT. MIDTOWN EAST STREET LOBBY - CONTINUOUS

WE PAN off sliding glass doors as MICHAEL HOFFMAN enters the lobby of the office building.

113 **INT. RUDOLPH HEYWOOD & ASSOCIATES LOBBY - MOMENTS LATER** 113

MICHAEL HOFFMAN approaches the firm's RECEPTIONIST.

> MICHAEL HOFFMAN
> Looking for Rudolph Heywood and Associates.

> RECEPTIONIST
> Beg your pardon, sir, but who is it that you're looking for?

> MICHAEL HOFFMAN
> László. Toth. He draws there.

She reviews a form in front of her.

> RECEPTIONIST
> Could I ask you to spell that? Oh, yes- I see him. Draftsmen are right upstairs.

114 **INT. RUDOLPH HEYWOOD & ASSOCIATES DRAWING ROOM - MOMENTS LATER** 114

WE STEADICAM up the stairs and across the space with MICHAEL HOFFMAN past thirty or so men with hair cut close to the scalp and short neckties all hunched over desks and easels.

PUSH IN ON LÁSZLÓ, who has aged and further decayed somewhat. He smokes a pipe at a drawing board. A green desk lamp highlights an inscrutable expression.

There's visible bruising, track marks, where his sleeves are rolled up.

115 **INT. LÁSZLÓ AND ERZSÉBET'S TENEMENT - KITCHEN - NIGHT** 115

ERZSÉBET and LÁSZLÓ sit across from ZSÓFIA and her husband, **BINYAMIN**, an orthodox Jewish man. **ZSÓFIA is five months pregnant and speaking again.**

> ZSÓFIA
> (soft-spoken)
> We have some news.

> LÁSZLÓ
> As do I.

> ERZSÉBET
> Oh, how exciting. What is it László?

> LÁSZLÓ
> Please. Zsófia, go ahead.

> ZSÓFIA
> We are making Aliyah.

ERZSÉBET looks a little heartbroken.

> ERZSÉBET
> What?

> ZSÓFIA
> We are going to Jerusalem.

> ERZSÉBET
> Yes, I heard you.

> ZSÓFIA
> Binyamin has family there.

BINYAMIN
My older brothers relocated with their families in 1950. They became citizens.

ERZSÉBET nods, considers this.

ERZSÉBET
Life is difficult there. Have you thought this through?

ZSÓFIA
It is our obligation.

LÁSZLÓ
To whom?

ZSÓFIA
Our repatriation is our liberation.

LÁSZLÓ swats at the air, starting to get worked up.

LÁSZLÓ
Where will you live? Where will you work?

BINYAMIN
We can stay with my brother's family when we first arrive.

ERZSÉBET silences LÁSZLÓ by resting her hand on his.

ERZSÉBET
I was planning to help with the baby.

BINYAMIN
My brother's wife can help, also.

ZSÓFIA
I am Jewish. My child is Jewish. It's time for us to go home.

ERZSÉBET snaps.

ERZSÉBET
Does it somehow make us less Jewish that we are _here_?

Silence.

ERZSÉBET (CONT'D)
Oh, I see, perhaps Binyamin did not recognize me to begin with—

ZSÓFIA
He does.

Beat.

ERZSÉBET
I'm sorry.

ZSÓFIA
No, I am sorry.

ERZSÉBET
No, it's wonderful news and we reacted badly out of self-interest. We are simply...

ERZSÉBET's voice cracks and she begins to cry.

ERZSÉBET (CONT'D)
-going to miss you.

ZSÓFIA
Well, we would like you to come.

ERZSÉBET wipes her tears away trying to pull herself together.

ERZSÉBET
Dear, we have jobs here.

ZSÓFIA
You can have a better job in Israel.

ERZSÉBET
I like my job!

ZSÓFIA
A woman's column. It's beneath you.

ERZSÉBET
I write for a paper and I'm paid for it! How many women my age could make the same claim?

There's a heavy silence.

ERZSÉBET (CONT'D)
(deadpan)
What's your news, László?

LÁSZLÓ
Harrison's asked me back.

ERZSÉBET looks up at him.

LÁSZLÓ (CONT'D)
Michael came by the office today. Insurance monies came through. They plan to forego the library to compensate for legal expenses but they want to complete the project.

ERZSÉBET
What about your job here at Heywood?

Silence.

                ERZSÉBET (CONT'D)
    You throw everything up in the air,
    just like that?

ERZSÉBET sulks.

                ERZSÉBET (CONT'D)
    I don't like that man.

                LÁSZLÓ
    You scarcely knew him.

                ERZSÉBET
    He dropped you as quickly as he
    took you on.

Beat.

                ERZSÉBET (CONT'D)
    You've already said yes, I take it?

No response.

                LÁSZLÓ
    He's in Roma on business and would
    like me to join him to review
    marbles for the altarpiece in
    Carrara.

                ERZSÉBET
    See! I told you that for him it's
    like doing a kitchen!

ERZSÉBET is embarrassed by their public dispute.

                ERZSÉBET (CONT'D)
    Everyone is leaving me.

                ZSÓFIA
    No, it isn't true.

                ERZSÉBET
    Isn't it?

                ZSÓFIA
    No. Uncle László is leaving you
    only a short time.

                LÁSZLÓ
    Some days.

                ZSÓFIA
    And I will visit and so will you.
    We will find a way.

                LÁSZLÓ
    I can arrange to have you dropped
    and picked up at the newspaper
    while I'm gone.

                    ERZSÉBET
          It's not just this trip. You'll be
          at Doylestown again now... I'll be
          fine on my own.

                    LÁSZLÓ
          I will make arrangements.

116   **INT. TENEMENT BUILDING - BEDROOM - NIGHT**   116

       ERZSÉBET holds on to LÁSZLÓ for dear life.

                    ERZSÉBET
          Promise you won't let it drive you
          mad.

                    LÁSZLÓ
          I promise.

117   **INT. TENEMENT BUILDING - BATHROOM - MORNING**   117

       In a small toiletry pouch with his shaving kit, LÁSZLÓ pulls
       out a small syringe and spoon. He makes an internal decision
       and dismantles the syringe, making it less recognizable at a
       glance. He tucks it back in the pouch for safe-keeping and
       places it in his luggage.

                    ERZSÉBET (O.S.)
          It's time to go! You'll be late!

                                                     CROSS DISSOLVE:

118   **EXT. CARRARA TOWN SQUARE - CAFE - DAY**   118

       A perfect portrait of VAN BUREN in a white suit.

       ANGLE ON -

       LÁSZLÓ and VAN BUREN sip coffees and smoke at an outdoor
       table, the sunlight is brilliant and white hot.

                    VAN BUREN
          I must say, Mr. Toth, you look a
          mess. I'd expect your Elizabeth to
          be taking better care of you.

                    LÁSZLÓ
          The years have been difficult.

                    VAN BUREN
          For us all! For us all!

       VAN BUREN regards his watch.

                    VAN BUREN (CONT'D)
          Where in the hell is he?

                    LÁSZLÓ
          I am sure he will be along any
          minute.

Beat.

                    VAN BUREN
          This is why I never do business
          with Italians. They are the spics
          of Europe.

LÁSZLÓ points.

                    LÁSZLÓ
          That's him.

ANGLE ON -

A middle-aged man, **ORAZIO**, on approach. He waves
enthusiastically at LÁSZLÓ.

                    ORAZIO
               (calls out)
          Ciao amico Laz-o!

ORAZIO reaches him and embraces him.

                    LÁSZLÓ
          Nice to see you.

He kisses LÁSZLÓ and extends his hand to VAN BUREN. ORAZIO is
missing two fingers on his right hand so he offers him his
left.

                    ORAZIO
          Orazio, a pleasure to meet you. I
          will take a quick coffee and we
          will go.

VAN BUREN nods. ORAZIO heads inside the cafe.

                    VAN BUREN
          What happened to his hand?

                    LÁSZLÓ
          Dangerous work-

119   **EXT. CARRARA MARBLE QUARRY - LATER**   119

Dramatic skies frame a sea of white marble. Shapes that
resemble small pueblos without entrances emerge from the
rock. Channeling machines pillage the earth, excavating
marble, Venato, Arabescato, and Cardoso stone. The air
whistles. The sun bears down.

HANDHELD ON -

VAN BUREN, ORAZIO and LÁSZLÓ walk across the massive lower
flatbed of the quarry. Colossal blocks of stone encircle
them.

                    ORAZIO
          You are tough, Mr. Laz-o, you know?
          Not so many people I see anymore
          from before the war.

                    VAN BUREN
          I've worn the wrong shoes for this
          trek. May, I take your arm László?

LÁSZLÓ takes VAN BUREN by the arm, steadying him.

                    ORAZIO
          Step where I step and you'll be all
          right.

ORAZIO leads them further and further.

                    ORAZIO (CONT'D)
          I'm not surprised to see you
          though! Some people; you just knew
          somehow they would be all right.
          You are stubborn! I am stubborn
          too. I am so stubborn, I never
          leave it here! I traveled only once
          in twenty years to Giulino, Azzano
          to beat the corpse of Mussolini
          with my own hands. Those of us
          here, my colleagues, we are
          anarchisti, the resistance. No one
          knows the quarries like us. We led
          members of the *Esercito Nazionale
          Repubblicano* into the caves here,
          captured them, dropped stones on
          them.

They come upon a beautiful alcove of dark stone.

                    ORAZIO (CONT'D)
          Here we are... It's beautiful, no?
          The channeling will be done here in
          one month. If you like it, we can
          have it fixed and ready for you in
          April.

VAN BUREN is once again enchanted. He walks all around it, presses his cheek to it. It's sensual, fetishistic.

                    VAN BUREN
          It's beautiful. Exactly as you
          described, László.

                    ORAZIO
          If you like, I tell the boys and we
          bring it to my atelier when the
          stone is cut.

                    LÁSZLÓ
          We like it.

120   **INT. ORAZIO'S ATELIER - NIGHT**   120

CUE: Mina's "*You are my destiny.*' The lively music blasts through the space, an echo chamber.

Surrounded by magnificent classical and modernistic sculptures in various stages of completion, a group of local artisans and masons drink copious amounts of digestivo at the back of the atelier and dance together. Everyone sings along in improper English.

                    EVERYONE
              (sings)
         *You are my destiny
         you are that's what to me
         You are my happiness
         That's what you are
         You have my sweet caress
         You share my loneliness
         You're more than life to me
         That's what you are
         Heaven and heaven alone
         Can take your love from me....*

ANGLE ON -

An entranced VAN BUREN observes LÁSZLÓ from the shadows.

LONG LENS ON -

LÁSZLÓ dances with girls and boys, exhilarated. He sings!

                    LÁSZLÓ
              (sings)
         *'Cause I'd be a fool
         To ever leave you dear
         And a fool I'd never be
         You are my destiny
         You share my reverie
         You're more than life to me
         That's what you are.*

LÁSZLÓ abruptly excuses himself from his dance partner and walks away from the group.

ANGLE ON -

VAN BUREN follows LÁSZLÓ with his eyes.

121   **INT. ORAZIO'S ATELIER - LATER**   121

VAN BUREN walks past a row of statues, looking for the toilet. He hears LÁSZLÓ breathing heavy and moves to investigate.

                    VAN BUREN
              (calls out)
         Mr. T-oth, it's time we return to
         our quarters. Orazio has kindly
         offered us a place to sleep for the
         night.

VAN BUREN turns to discover LÁSZLÓ slouched against a wide marble column in a terrible state, an unspooled pouch of hop gear in his lap... His eyes have rolled back in his head. He's barely responsive.

                    VAN BUREN (CONT'D)
              What have you done to yourself?

VAN BUREN slides his back down the column and sits next to him displaying a casual air.

                    VAN BUREN (CONT'D)
              It's a shame seeing how your people
              treat themselves. If you resent
              your persecution, why then do you
              make of yourself such an easy
              target?

LÁSZLÓ cannot respond.

                    VAN BUREN (CONT'D)
              If you act as a loafer living off
              handouts, a societal leech, how can
              you rightfully expect a different
              result? You have so much potential
              and yet you squander it.

LÁSZLÓ starts to vomit and VAN BUREN moves in behind him, pats him on the back.

                    VAN BUREN (CONT'D)
              Get it out. Get it out, my friend.

Below frame, VAN BUREN fusses with his belt. LÁSZLÓ gags and coughs.

                    VAN BUREN (CONT'D)
              It's all right, my boy. Get it out.

VAN BUREN systematically pulls down LÁSZLÓ's pants below frame. He spits, and thrusts.

                    VAN BUREN (CONT'D)
                    (whispers, slurs)
              Who do you think you are? You think
              you're special? You think you float
              directly above everyone you
              encounter because you are
              beautiful? Because you are
              educated?

LONG LENS ON -

LÁSZLÓ's face is pressed against the ground. He's too strung out to defend himself. His eyes widen in terror.

                    VAN BUREN (O.S.) (CONT'D)
              You're a tramp. Shh. You're a lady
              of the night.

The assault is brief but clear.

                                        FADE TO BLACK.

122   **EXT. CARRARA MARBLE QUARRY - DAY**   122

White heat. The searing image is overexposed by two stops.

HANDHELD ON -

LÁSZLÓ walks and stumbles behind his abuser who ascends the quarry trail ahead of him. Never turning to face him, VAN BUREN recounts...

>   VAN BUREN
>   (calls out)
>   You were in quite a state last
>   night. Orazio carried you to bed!

VAN BUREN hums Mina's "*You are my destiny.*'

>   VAN BUREN (CONT'D)
>   It's a 4 hour train to the airport
>   in Fiumicino so you have time for a
>   rest. I hope your stomach isn't too
>   sensitive on aeroplanes!

123 **INT. TENEMENT BUILDING - KITCHEN - DAY** 123

CLOSE ON -

ERZSÉBET composes a letter to her niece in an elegant script. A few banknotes sit in a pile to the side.

>   ERZSÉBET (V.O.)
>   *My dearest Zsófia!*
>   *Mazel tov! She is so beautiful -*
>   *your spitting image!*

124 **EXT. VISTA - CONSTRUCTION SITE - DAY** 124

ULTRA-FAST MOTION -

Back in Doylestown, much time has passed. The site is active, abuzz again.

>   ERZSÉBET (V.O.)
>   *Don't be mad but your Uncle László*
>   *insisted I enclose a few banknotes*
>   *for you and Binyamin. We hope he*
>   *won't be offended, and that it's*
>   *not too difficult to change these*
>   *into the local currency.*

VARIOUS ANGLES ON -

- Cargo is unloaded.

- A cement mixer turns fresh concrete.

- Cement floors are polished.

- Grids of scaffolding are erected.

- Tarps are pulled over church pews in the rain.

- A large clock inside the institute ticks towards noon.

- A SLOW TILT and PAN across a cement dome.

125   **INT. INSTITUTE STAIRWELL - CONSTRUCTION SITE - DUSK**   125

SFX: DIEGETIC AUDIO IS MUTE.

WE STEADICAM with LÁSZLÓ and his nemesis, JIM SIMPSON, older now, marching up a staircase through the action on-site. LÁSZLÓ and JIM SIMPSON feverishly argue but ERZSÉBET's voice-over drowns out all diegetic audio.

>   ERZSÉBET (V.O.)
>   *Here: I am so alone. Perhaps more
>   alone than I have ever been. Your
>   uncle has closed a door to me. The
>   man I married is inside but the
>   lock's combination, I cannot
>   decipher...*

126   **EXT. VISTA - CONSTRUCTION SITE - DUSK**   126

STEADICAM ON -

LÁSZLÓ walks with a lamp closely observing the freshly laid concrete for the cistern

>   ERZSÉBET (V.O.)
>   *He no longer attends synagogue.
>   When I ask him why, he will not
>   reply. Perhaps his own narcissism
>   will no longer allow him a
>   relationship with our community.*

LÁSZLÓ ascends a staircase and arrives out of the darkness to a picturesque sky to find...

>   ERZSÉBET (V.O.)
>   *Tell me how you are. How you really
>   are. All our love and warmth to the
>   three of you.
>   Erzsébet*

WE PAN to an exposed staircase on the horizon that leads to nowhere.

127   **EXT. VISTA - CONSTRUCTION SITE - DAY**   127

LÁSZLÓ stands with a small group of employees explaining a nuanced architectural detail.

>   LÁSZLÓ
>   You see this, above us?

There's a four inch gap between flats allowing sunlight to seep through above them.

                    LÁSZLÓ (CONT'D)
          Measure the same distance of three
          or perhaps four inches between
          flats, and place each modular
          section apart by that same
          distance.

The CONSTRUCTION SUPERVISOR interjects...

                    CONSTRUCTION SUPERVISOR
          This isn't supposed to stay like
          this though. We just set it here
          for approximate placement.

LÁSZLÓ obsessively explains...

                    LÁSZLÓ
          I know it's not supposed to stay
          like this but keep it like this- I
          like it like this.

                    CONSTRUCTION SUPERVISOR
          What do we do with those gaps?

                    LÁSZLÓ
          We insert a thick sheet of glass
          between them to let the light in
          from above- give me some time to
          think about it and I come back to
          you.

LÁSZLÓ sees something in the distance which catches his attention.

ANGLE ON -

ERZSÉBET visits the site. GORDON, visibly older, pushes the chair.

LONG LENS ON -

A **YOUNG EMPLOYEE** does pull ups on some scaffolding that's set up around the base of the clock tower. The other young men above him count down.

                    CONSTRUCTION CREW
                (cheering him on)
          Twenty! Nineteen! Eighteen!
          Seventeen.

LÁSZLÓ comes upon them.

                    LÁSZLÓ
                (shouts)
          YOU ALL STOP THAT RIGHT NOW. WHAT'S
          YOUR NAME? Are you trying to pull
          the thing down and get them all
          killed?!

The YOUNG EMPLOYEE's response is inaudible.

LÁSZLÓ (CONT'D)
Your childish show-boating puts everyone else here at risk! Are you thick?! Are you lame?! You report to the subcontractor. You tell him that you've been let go.

A concerned ERZSÉBET observes her husband shouting at the YOUNG EMPLOYEE. She looks up at Gordon.

ERZSÉBET
Gordon, can you get him to stop shouting at everyone?

LONG LENS ON -

The YOUNG EMPLOYEE starts to walk off, seemingly mutters something under his breath. **An infuriated LÁSZLÓ runs after the boy and kicks his behind.** The gesture is equal parts absurd and harrowing.

GORDON intervenes...

GORDON
What's the problem here?

LÁSZLÓ
It's already taken care of.

GORDON
You kicked that boy.

LÁSZLÓ
Stay out of it, Gordon.

GORDON
What's wrong with you?

LÁSZLÓ
(shouts)
Stay out of it, I said, or you can go with him!

GORDON
(affirmative)
You shout at me again and you'll be sorry.

LÁSZLÓ considers this, swallows, then doubles down...

LÁSZLÓ
(shouts)
You too! Get out of here.

LÁSZLÓ marches toward ERZSÉBET leaving GORDON behind him.

LÁSZLÓ (CONT'D)
(calls out)
Let's go home.

ERZSÉBET
I only just arrived!

JIM SIMPSON enters the frame, on a mission, approaching
LÁSZLÓ with a stack of paperwork.

> JIM SIMPSON
> Mr. Toth, you and I need to talk
> through these May/June cost
> reports.

LÁSZLÓ throws a hand up in the air to block out the nuisance.

> LÁSZLÓ
> Not today, Jim!

> JIM SIMPSON
> You can't just walk away every time
> I step into a room, Mr. Toth!

LÁSZLÓ is maniacally defiant.

> LÁSZLÓ
> Honey, have I introduced you to Jim
> Simpson? Jim is the boss' lap dog
> and *Architectural Consultant
> Extraordinaire*! He designed a hotel
> in Stamford.

> ERZSÉBET
> László, that's enough!

> LÁSZLÓ
> There must be an unpaid parking
> meter around here somewhere, Jimmy!
> Be vigilant! Keep your eyes peeled!

128 **INT. AUTOMOBILE - EVENING**   128

LÁSZLÓ and ERZSÉBET are en route back to Manhattan. There is
a palpable tension between them. LÁSZLÓ breaks the silence.

> LÁSZLÓ
> (cold)
> What is it?

> ERZSÉBET
> It was unnecessary how you treated
> that boy is all.

> LÁSZLÓ
> Their safety is my priority.

> ERZSÉBET
> (despondent)
> And Gordon, don't even get me
> started.

ERZSÉBET thinks, continues...

> ERZSÉBET (CONT'D)
> It is not what you said to that
> young man, it is *how*.

LÁSZLÓ
Would you like us to wait around another few years for *another* lawsuit to resolve itself? I am SICK of it. Do you hear me?!

Beat.

LÁSZLÓ (CONT'D)
I finish THIS or WE are finished.

ERZSÉBET shouts.

ERZSÉBET
Speak for yourself! I am NOT finished. Living with you is *impossible*. You've become a selfish old bastard right before my very eyes!

LÁSZLÓ
Don't say something you'll regret in the morning.

ERZSÉBET hits him hard causing the car to swerve.

LÁSZLÓ (CONT'D)
You want to kill us?

ERZSÉBET
I'd get out of the car and march all the way back to Manhattan if I could, you egotistic scoundrel. There is NO REASON for me to be here. I am here for you! I could do my ridiculous job ANYWHERE! Do you think I went to university to write about lipsticks! Shame on you.

LÁSZLÓ
WE CAME BECAUSE IT WAS OUR ONLY OPTION! Attila was here-

ERZSÉBET
WHO YOU REFUSE TO SEE!

LÁSZLÓ
Ask him about that. Did he tell you that he kicked me to the street like a dog?

She is silent.

LÁSZLÓ (CONT'D)
His bitch wife accused me of making a pass at her.

ERZSÉBET
You would never do that.

LÁSZLÓ
I did NOT do that.

ERZSÉBET
Why would she say such a thing?

LÁSZLÓ
Because they do not want us here.

ERZSÉBET
Of course Attila wants us here.

LÁSZLÓ
Not Attila.

ERZSÉBET
Who do you mean?

LÁSZLÓ
The people here, they do not want us here. Audrey, Attila's *Catholic wife* DOES NOT WANT US HERE. We are nothing. Worse than nothing.

ERZSÉBET weeps.

ERZSÉBET
You poor man. My poor husband. What's been robbed of you-

129 **INT. TENEMENT BUILDING - BEDROOM - NIGHT** 129

ERZSÉBET howls in pain, a recurring night terror.

ERZSÉBET
(cries out)
Zsófia!

LÁSZLÓ tries to calm her.

LÁSZLÓ
She's gone, darling. She isn't here. You must calm yourself. You've worked yourself up is all.

ERZSÉBET
I am in pain. I am close to death.

LÁSZLÓ
You are not. I am so sorry I upset you.

ERZSÉBET weeps trembles. It's like an exorcism.

ERZSÉBET
Get me my pills, it's too much.

130 **INT. TENEMENT BUILDING - BATHROOM - CONTINUOUS** 130

HANDHELD ON -

The energy is frantic. She's wailing in the other room. He rifles through the medicine cabinet, opens her pill box. A half a pill drops out of an otherwise empty bottle.

> LÁSZLÓ
> (calls out)
> There is only a pill, cut in halves! Do you keep some in your purse?

She cries out again in pain.

131   **INT. TENEMENT BUILDING - BEDROOM - MOMENTS LATER**   131

LÁSZLÓ enters.

> LÁSZLÓ
> There is only half. Do you keep more in your purse?

ERZSÉBET shakes her head.

> ERZSÉBET
> (weeps)
> What will I do? The pain won't stop coming.

132   **INT. TENEMENT BUILDING - BATHROOM - CONTINUOUS**   132

BIRD'S-EYE VIEW ON -

LÁSZLÓ re-enters. He pulls down his toiletry pouch from the top of the medicine cabinet. He pulls out a spoon and dropper.

133   **INT. TENEMENT BUILDING - BEDROOM - MOMENTS LATER**   133

ERZSÉBET writhes on the bed. LÁSZLÓ enters.

> LÁSZLÓ
> I found something.

She can't respond. He sits beside her and prepares a vein.

> LÁSZLÓ (CONT'D)
> It's what they gave me on the boat for my broken face-

He makes the injection.

> LÁSZLÓ (CONT'D)
> Shh. You'll feel better soon, just listen to my voice, dear.

A trance-like calm comes over her. He then prepares himself a dose.

CROSS DISSOLVE:

134   **INT. TENEMENT BUILDING - BEDROOM - MORNING**   134

LÁSZLÓ lies in his wife's arms like a child. The light is beautiful. He looks up at her. She's like an angel.

                  ERZSÉBET
                (whispers)
          Do you have more?

135   **INT. TENEMENT BUILDING - KITCHEN - LATER**   135

LÁSZLÓ closes the blinds to keep out the harsh afternoon sunlight.

136   **INT. TENEMENT BUILDING - BEDROOM - LATER**   136

The room is very dark. The two of them make love. A cock, an elbow, an arched back. An intense, physical dream.

                  LÁSZLÓ
                (Hungarian)
          I love you.

                  ERZSÉBET
          Keep going. Harder.

Score for Piano gives the sequence warmth, a strange feeling.

137   **INT. TENEMENT BUILDING - BEDROOM - LATER**   137

She's completely out of it, moans.

                  ERZSÉBET
         Toilet-

LÁSZLÓ stands starts to scoop her in his arms.

                                JUMP CUT TO:

138   **INT. TENEMENT BUILDING - BATHROOM - CONTINUOUS**   138

He clumsily finishes placing her on the toilet seat.

                  LÁSZLÓ
         I'll wait outside. Tell me when you need me.

                                JUMP CUT TO:

139   **INT. TENEMENT BUILDING - BEDROOM - MOMENTS LATER**   139

LÁSZLÓ leans against the wall. After a moment...

                    LÁSZLÓ
            Darling, have you finished?

No response. After a beat, he knocks...

                    LÁSZLÓ (CONT'D)
            Can I come in?

He opens the door... **ERZSÉBET is foaming at the mouth.**

                                        HARD CUT TO:

140   **EXT. MANHATTAN HOSPITAL - NIGHT**   140

LÁSZLÓ runs carrying his wife like a rag doll.

                    LÁSZLÓ
            HELP! Someone help me! My wife is
            dying!

A smoking nurse rushes to his aid.

                    LÁSZLÓ (CONT'D)
            Please help her, she's dying.

                    NURSE
            She's breathing.

In his current state, he's like a child mourning a parental
loss.

                    LÁSZLÓ
            I know my wife. She is dying.

                    NURSE
                (calls out to someone off-
                 screen)
            Get us a wheelchair, a gurney,
            anything!

He reverts to Hungarian, weeps.

                    LÁSZLÓ
                (Hungarian)
            I am sorry.

141   **EXT. VISTA - CONSTRUCTION SITE - DAWN**   141

The Marble Altarpiece is unwrapped by CREWMEN from Shibari-
style knots and canvas. After some time, ERZSÉBET's voice
fades in over the transcendent image.

                    ERZSÉBET (O.S.)
                (weak)
            Last night, I met God and he
            granted me permission to call him
            by his name. It is not the first
            time we have met.

BEAT.

                    ERZSÉBET (CONT'D)
          What did you do to me, my László?

SILENCE.

                    LÁSZLÓ (O.S.)
                (holds back tears)
          It was an accident.

142   **INT. HOSPITAL ROOM - DAWN**   142

        Fans swing on their hinges. The space is a long corridor fit
        with 12 beds. ERZSÉBET is alive but exhausted.

                    ERZSÉBET
          Do you remember everything you
          confessed to me at home in our bed?

        LÁSZLÓ shakes his head, ashamed.

                    ERZSÉBET (CONT'D)
          You needn't be ashamed, my darling.
          The harm done unto us were done
          only to our physical bodies.

        She smiles, laughs.

                    ERZSÉBET (CONT'D)
          You were right. This place is
          rotten. The landscape. The food we
          eat. This whole country is rotten.

        She strokes his hand.

                    ERZSÉBET (CONT'D)
          I'm going to Israel to be with
          Zsófia and her child. I want to
          become the grandmother to her that
          she will, otherwise, never
          encounter.

        LÁSZLÓ cries.

                    ERZSÉBET (CONT'D)
          Come home with me.

                    LÁSZLÓ
          I will follow you until I die.

        HOLD ON LÁSZLÓ... Softer, more beautiful than ever.

                                                    CROSS DISSOLVE:

143   **EXT. VAN BUREN ESTATE - GATES - EVENING**   143

ERZSÉBET arrives by a Philadelphia Taxi Service. The main gates are closed so ERZSÉBET must go on foot. Her driver steps out and helps her arrange herself with a walker.

144   **EXT. VAN BUREN ESTATE - DRIVEWAY - MOMENTS LATER**   144

HANDHELD ON-

ERZSÉBET breathes hard, audibly grievous, makes her way up to the front door with her walker at a fairly steady clip.

145   **INT. VAN BUREN ESTATE - FOYER - LATER**   145

NOTE: The following sequence is in one unbroken take until otherwise noted.

ERZSÉBET waits in the hallway, she dabs her forehead with her handkerchief exhausted from the walk. After a moment, MAGGIE LEE enters to welcome her.

>   MAGGIE LEE
>   Mrs. Toth! How lovely to see you!
>   Do you need a hand?

>   ERZSÉBET
>   I'm all right, thank you.

>   MAGGIE LEE
>   Is Mr. Toth here, as well?

>   ERZSÉBET
>   Just me, I'm afraid.

>   MAGGIE LEE
>   To what do we owe the pleasure?

>   ERZSÉBET
>   Is your father in?

>   MAGGIE LEE
>   We were just sitting down to
>   dinner.

>   ERZSÉBET
>   No trouble at all. I'm happy to
>   wait until you're all finished.

MAGGIE LEE furrows her brow.

>   MAGGIE LEE
>   Don't be silly! I'll have the
>   kitchen fix you a plate.

>   ERZSÉBET
>   You're kind, Maggie, thank you.

MAGGIE LEE
Right this way.

ERZSÉBET turns and follows MAGGIE LEE ten meters to the dining room where she finds...

146   **INT. VAN BUREN ESTATE - DINING ROOM - CONTINUOUS**   146

VAN BUREN and HARRY LEE are seated at the table. A few UNRECOGNIZABLE ASSOCIATES are present, as well. They all rise to greet her.

ERZSÉBET
Please sit.

HARRY LEE
Mrs. Toth, you're up on your feet!

VAN BUREN regards her.

VAN BUREN
Where is László?

ERZSÉBET
He's caught a flu. He's recovering at home.

HARRY LEE
That explains it! Jim Simpson mentioned he hadn't been on-site since last Friday.

VAN BUREN
Shame.

ERZSÉBET
(cold)
Yes. A terrible shame.

HARRY LEE
It's going around. Please, sit down.

ERZSÉBET refuses to sit.

ERZSÉBET
I'm fine to stand.

HARRY LEE
Fine to stand? Is something wrong, Mrs. Toth?

ERZSÉBET
Yes, something is wrong.

The blood runs cold.

ERZSÉBET (CONT'D)
I've come tonight to tell you something that is going to be very difficult to hear.

VAN BUREN shoots a look at her.

> ERZSÉBET (CONT'D)
> And for you people too. I don't know you but it will be difficult for you to hear.

> HARRY LEE
> If this is a professional matter then perhaps you and I should talk in the other room.

HARRY stands.

> ERZSÉBET
> (calm, resolute)
> Your father is a rapist.

> HARRY LEE
> Excuse me - whatever this is supposed to be, I don't like it. I'm calling your husband to come and fetch you.

> ERZSÉBET
> Your father is an evil rapist.

MAGGIE LEE believes her. HARRY rushes her.

> MAGGIE LEE
> Don't push her, Harry!

VAN BUREN is silent.

> ERZSÉBET
> Look at him. He cannot say anything.

> MAGGIE LEE
> Daddy, has something happened between you and Mrs. Toth?

> ERZSÉBET
> It wasn't me-

> HARRY LEE
> (shouts)
> That's enough. You come in here making vague, laughable accusations! I want you out of our house this instant.

> ERZSÉBET
> Tell them what you did to my husband. Tell them what you did.

MAGGIE covers her face, horrified by the accusation.

> VAN BUREN
> Your husband is sick. He is an alcoholic and a drug addict. I don't know why he wishes to hurt me, humiliate me.
> (MORE)

                    VAN BUREN (CONT'D)
          I have offered him nothing but
          kindness. He's a sick, senile old
          dog and when dogs get sick, they
          often bite the hand that's fed them
          before someone mercifully puts them
          down.

VAN BUREN stands.

                    VAN BUREN (CONT'D)
          Now, if you'll excuse me, I've
          withstood enough abuse for one
          evening. You can tell your husband
          he's off the payroll now and
          forever, as well.

ERZSÉBET explodes.

                    ERZSÉBET
          I WILL NOT EXCUSE YOU!

HARRY starts violently dragging her out of the room.

                    MAGGIE LEE
               (shouts)
          Stop it, Harry!

                    ERZSÉBET
          YOU ARE NOT EXCUSED, HARRISON VAN
          BUREN!

HARRY muscles her all the way to the foyer.

147   **INT. VAN BUREN ESTATE - FOYER - LATER**   147

He drags her all the way to the front door where she falls.

                    MAGGIE LEE (O.S.)
               (shouts)
          Stop it, Harry!

                    ERZSÉBET
          SHAME! SHAME ON YOU!

MAGGIE LEE screams from off-screen and comes running to
ERZSÉBET's aid.

                    ERZSÉBET (CONT'D)
          I'm fine, Maggie. I'm fine. Can you
          help me to my car? A taxi's waiting
          for me at the front.

HARRY LEE opens the door and sets her walker outside.

                    HARRY LEE
          You never come back here, you crazy
          woman.

MAGGIE gets ERZSÉBET to her feet. They stumble to the front
door and exit. HARRY LEE exhales, paces back and forth, then
walks back to the dining room. The camera follows...

148   **INT. VAN BUREN ESTATE - DINING ROOM - CONTINUOUS**   148

The guests are standing to leave.

>   HARRY LEE
>   I am so sorry for the bizarre
>   interruption.

>   GUEST
>   It's all right, Harry. We'll leave.

>   HARRY LEE
>   Don't leave yet. Please.

>   GUEST
>   Your father's gone to bed.

He turns on his shoe.

149   **INT. VAN BUREN ESTATE - FOYER - CONTINUOUS**   149

HARRY LEE walks back again the way he came.

>   HARRY LEE
>   (shouts)
>   Father! It's over now. She's gone!

HARRY LEE turns a corner-

150   **INT. VAN BUREN ESTATE - STAIRWELL - CONTINUOUS**   150

-and moves up the stairwell.

151   **INT. VAN BUREN ESTATE - CORRIDOR - CONTINUOUS**   151

He walks down the hallway to his father's bedroom at the end of the hall. He opens his father's door. The room is empty... He turns back the way he came then stops at his father's study. It's empty, as well.

>   HARRY LEE
>   (shouts)
>   Dad!

He opens every door on the floor. Nothing. Nothing. Nothing.

>   MAGGIE LEE (O.S.)
>   Is he not upstairs?

>   HARRY LEE
>   (shouts)
>   Where the hell has he gone? Call
>   for him outside.

152	**INT. VAN BUREN ESTATE - STAIRWELL - CONTINUOUS**	152

He starts back down the stairs, increasingly panicked.

153	**INT. VAN BUREN ESTATE - FOYER - CONTINUOUS**	153

He crosses to the front door and exits to the driveway.

154	**EXT. VAN BUREN ESTATE - DRIVEWAY**	154

He calls out with increasing desperation for his father.

>   HARRY LEE
>   (shouts)
>   DAD!
>
>   MAGGIE LEE (O.S.)
>   *DADDY?! Can you hear us?!*

NOTE: End of continuous take.

155	**EXT. VAN BUREN ESTATE - FOREST - DAWN**	155

ULTRA-WIDE ON -

Snow falls on a **search team** made up of LOCAL VOLUNTEERS; each individual spread 10 meters apart combs the area for any sign of VAN BUREN.

>   LOCAL VOLUNTEERS
>   *HARRISON!*

156	**EXT. VISTA - CONSTRUCTION SITE - DUSK**	156

The austere beauty of LÁSZLÓ's design is revealed through the following series of angles...

- TRACK RIGHT with the volunteers as they move across the site navigating these modern ruins.

157	**EXT. INSTITUTE CORRIDORS - SAME**	157

VARIOUS SHOTS -

The search party use flashlights to investigate the institute...

158	**INT. CISTERN - SAME**	158

WE TRACK BEHIND a group of volunteers as they walk the perimeter of the **RAINWATER HARVESTING SYSTEM** below grade.

LOCAL VOLUNTEERS
HARRISON!

159 **INT. CHAPEL - SAME** 159

WE PUSH IN ON a single volunteer as she walks past the marble altarpiece. It's a thing of extraordinary beauty.

VOLUNTEER (O.S.)
We've got something down here!

The sun forms a sign of the cross as LÁSZLÓ so frequently demonstrated in his model, and WE TILT UP to snow falling from above which has blown in from outside.

INSERT TITLE:

160 160

EPILOGUE
THE FIRST ARCHITECTURE BIENNALE
VENICE, ITALY 1980

FADE IN:

161 **EXT. VENICE, ITALY - EVENING** 161

A SERIES OF ANGLES establish the city of Venice in the evening.

162 **INT. GIARDINI - ARCHITECTURE BIENNALE - NIGHT** 162

A lavish Opening Night Gala event is in full swing. A small crowd is gathering around the Giardini's Israeli Pavilion.

163 **INT. CENTRAL PAVILION - MAIN GALLERY - SAME** 163

WE TRACK LEFT with a middle-aged woman (ZSÓFIA) pushing an elderly man (LÁSZLÓ) in a wheelchair. They pass row after row of ornate architectural models.

ZSÓFIA
They look beautiful like this, don't you think?

LÁSZLÓ nods, too frail to speak.

164 **INT. CENTRAL PAVILION - SOUTH GALLERY - MOMENTS LATER** 164

LÁSZLÓ puts his hand up to stop ZSÓFIA from exiting the room. He observes a projection of a macro-tour of his model work playing large on the gallery wall.

                        ZSÓFIA
            The director would like to speak
            with you before the ceremony. We
            should go.

165   **INT. ISRAELI PAVILION - LATER**   165

ZSÓFIA cries through her speech.

                        ZSÓFIA
            My uncle is, above all, a
            principled artist. His lifelong
            ambition was not only to define an
            epoch but to transcend all *time*.

She smiles.

                        ZSÓFIA (CONT'D)
            In his memoirs, he described his
            designs as machines with no
            superfluous parts, that at their
            best, at *his* best, possessed an
            immoveable core; a *"Hard Core of
            Beauty."*

ANGLE ON -

A variety of models for both unrealized and actualized
projects. The floor is littered with his life's work.

                        ZSÓFIA (CONT'D)
            A way of directing their
            inhabitant's perception to the
            world as it is. The inherent laws
            of concrete things such as
            mountains and rock define them.
            They indicate nothing. They tell
            nothing. They simply are.

BACK TO -

ZSÓFIA changes course.

                        ZSÓFIA (CONT'D)
            Born in 1911 in a small fishing
            village in *Austria-Hungary*, László
            Toth looked out upon the Adriatic
            Sea. He was a boy with eyes wide
            open, full of yearning. New borders
            would eventually rip this expanse
            of sea away from him but never did
            he cease to try and fill its void.

ZSÓFIA refers to her notes.

                        ZSÓFIA (CONT'D)
            Forty years later, he survived the
            camps at Buchenwald, as did his
            late wife, and myself, in Dachau.
            His first American masterpiece, the
            Van Buren institute outside of
            Philadelphia, remained unfinished
            until 1973.
                        (MORE)

ZSÓFIA (CONT'D)
          The building referenced his time at
          Buchenwald as well as the deeply
          felt absence of his wife, my Aunt
          Erzsébet.

ANGLE ON -

Architectural models of Buchenwald, Dachau, and the Van Buren
institute, side-by-side. The Biennale exhibit display their
similarities and differences.

                    ZSÓFIA (O.S.) (CONT'D)
          For this project, he re-imagined
          the camp's claustrophobic interior
          cells with precisely the same
          dimensions as his own place of
          imprisonment, save for one
          electrifying exception; when
          visitors looked 20 meters upwards,
          the dramatic heights of the glass
          above them invited free thought;
          freedom of identity. He further re-
          imagined Buchenwald and his wife's
          venue of imprisonment in Dachau on
          the same grounds, connected by a
          myriad of corridors-

PUSH IN ON ZSÓFIA -

                    ZSÓFIA (CONT'D)
          -re-writing their history and
          transcending space and time so that
          he and Erzsébet would _never_ be
          apart again.

ZSÓFIA concludes by looking directly at her uncle in the main
row...

                    ZSÓFIA (CONT'D)
                (smiles and weeps)
          Uncle, you and Aunt Erzsébet once
          spoke for me, I speak for you now,
          and I am honored.

Her voice cracks with heartbreak.

                    ZSÓFIA (CONT'D)
          "Don't let anyone fool you, Zsófia"
          he would say to me as a struggling
          young mother during our first years
          in Jerusalem, "no matter what the
          others try and sell you, it is _the
          destination_, not the journey."

**HOLD ON LÁSZLÓ, a man at the end of his life at the beginning
of a new epoch.**

Printed in Great Britain
by Amazon